MEXICO IN 22 DAYS

A STEP-BY-STEP GUIDE AND TRAVEL ITINERARY

BY STEVE ROGERS
AND TINA ROSA

PREFACE BY CARL FRANZ

For Maki & Muriel

Library of Congress Catalog No. 86-043069
All rights reserved.

Published by
John Muir Publications
Santa Fe, New Mexico
Printed in U.S.A.

Maps   Jim Wood
Cover   Tim Clark
Design/Production   Mary Shapiro
Typography   Copygraphics, Inc.
Editorial   Carl Franz and Richard Harris

ISBN 0-912528-64-8

CONTENTS

Preface by Carl Franz   4
How to Use This Book   6
Itinerary   15
Day 1   Arrive in Mexico City   18
Day 2   Explore Mexico City   25
Day 3   Mexico City and Teotihuacan   28
Day 4   San Miguel de Allende   34
Day 5   San Miguel de Allende   40
Day 6   Guanajuato   43
Day 7   Guanajuato—Patzcuaro   50
Day 8   Patzcuaro—Janitzio—Mexico City   54
Day 9   Oaxaca   56
Day 10   Tlacolula & Ruins   62
Day 11   Oaxaca—Monte Alban   64
Day 12   Travel to San Cristobal   69
Day 13   San Cristobal de las Casas   72
Day 14   Travel to Palenque   75
Day 15   Palenque   77
Day 16   Palenque—Merida   82
Day 17   Merida   86
Day 18   Chichen Itza   89
Day 19   Isla Mujeres   94
Day 20   Isla Mujeres   96
Day 21   Xel-Ha and Tulum   97
Day 22   Coba—Return to Merida   100
Post-Tour Options   102
Mexico City   102
Taxco   104
Pacific Beaches   105
Practical Extras   107
Culture Shock   107
Speaking Spanish   107
Mexican Food   113
Crafts and Folk Art   120
Fiestas   122
Weather   125
About the Authors   126

PREFACE
BY CARL FRANZ

Reading *Mexico in 22 Days* brought back a rush of memories from my first trip in 1964, when Steve tempted me out of college with an offer I couldn't refuse: a tour of a distant country called Mexico. It was an eye-opening and unforgettable experience, a non-stop series of exotic sights and adventures that would eventually lead me to a career as a travel writer.

Throughout that trip—which roughly followed this book's 22-day itinerary—Steve treated me to his famous "Mexico monologue," an empassioned, off-the-cuff travelogue punctuated by "Look at that!", "Did you see *that?*" and "I'll bet you didn't know that . . ." His interest in Mexico was all-consuming and highly contagious. No detail was allowed to escape my attention, and I can still feel Steve's elbow in my ribs as he gleefully pointed out yet another stunning view, quaint burro or picturesque colonial ruin. Meals became rest stops, with Steve eagerly poring over the menu as if it were a treasure map, urging me to sample the *cochinita pibil* rather than the more familiar chicken tacos, the *huachinango* rather than the club sandwich.

Our curiosity about Mexico, and the hospitality of the people we met along the way, gradually drew us deeper and deeper into the country. It wasn't long before our road map was thumbed beyond repair and our guidebooks were exhuasted. A trip that began as a lark was now an odyssey. We traveled from the ordinary to the unexpected, from the unusual to the outrageous. "This is *it!*" Steve cried. "This is the real Mexico!"

As I learned on my first trip, Mexico is a huge and diverse country. It's distinct foreignness, however, can be an obstacle as well as an attraction, even for the experienced traveler.

No wonder, then, that so many people throw their hands into the air when it comes time to decide: *How, when and where do we begin?* With Puerto Vallarta or Coatzacoalcos? Shall we explore the ruined cities of Coba and Chichen Itza or get lazy on the beaches of Oaxaca? Does anyone know when the train leaves for Lake Patzcuaro?

Mexico in 22 Days has the answers, along with a figurative elbow-in-the-ribs as Steve and Tina share both their enthusiasm for Mexico and comprehensive, up-to-date advice on everything from their favorite hotels to shopping tips for Indian textiles. Travelers will find a detailed, do-it-yourself itinerary combined with the kind of personal advice and "Look at that!" encouragement that makes this a genuine guide rather than just another directory of well-known sights.

Steve and Tina's suggested 22-day itinerary covers Mexico from Baja to the Yucatan, with never a dull moment in between. If you find yourself frazzled by the pace, slow down. When you discover a place you can't bear to leave, *don't*. For many people, the true pleasures of travel are found in getting to know a few places well, rather than globetrotting from Point A to Z.

Whatever your preference, *Mexico in 22 Days* is easily adapted to your own budget and style of travel. Use the book as a start-to-finish travel plan or take it area-by-area, as an excellent "wish list" of Mexico's classic and yet-to-be-discovered sights.

Explore Mexico for yourself and you'll discover, as so many of us have, that the excitement never ends.

—Carl Franz
October 1986

When Tina first went to Mexico from New York she was planning on a two week holiday. It took her 8 years to get back to New York. If this is your first trip to Mexico, be warned! It may be the beginning of a long love affair.

HOW TO USE THIS BOOK

This book is your pocket-sized "tour guide." It provides you the travel efficiency of an organized tour along with the freedom and flexibility that independent travelers enjoy.

Mexico in 22 Days presents a tried and proven itinerary for sampling the best that Mexico has to offer—ancient ruins, Indian marketplaces, colonial history, tropical beaches and lots more—with maximum value for your travel dollar.

Like every good itinerary, it also allows for change according to your personal interests and whims. Customize this itinerary and make it your own. Make changes. Take a pencil and draw lines through some sentences, circles around others; scribble notes in the margins. As you talk with other travelers, refine your plan further. Spend more time in the places that intrigue you and skip those that don't. If a place bores you, leave early, substitute a side trip or schedule an extra day on the beach.

In the 22 "Days" you'll find:

1. An **Introductory Overview** for each day.

2. An hour-by-hour **Suggested Schedule** for each day.

3. A list of **Sightseeing Highlights** (rated: ▲▲▲ Don't miss; ▲▲ Try hard to see; ▲ Worthwhile if you can make it).

4. **Transportation** tips and instructions, including self-guided **Walking Tours** of sightseeing highlights.

5. **Food** and **Accommodations**: How and where to find the best places in your price range, including addresses, phone numbers and our favorites.

6. **Orientation** and an easy-to-read **Map** of the area.

7. **Helpful Hints** on shopping and other incidents of Mexican travel.

8. **In-Tour Extensions** for those who have more time. Suggestions for exploring the area in more depth.

At the end of the book you'll find chapters presenting **practical information** and **cultural insights** to enhance your trip.

How Much Will This Trip Cost?

Mexico's inflation rate is astounding to many Americans. So is the declining value of the peso, which translates into *increasing* value of the US dollar. All this economic see-sawing makes travel costs in Mexico unpredictable, but we'll stick our necks out and hazard some rough "guestimates."

These price estimates are based on two people traveling together and sharing hotel rooms. The actual "per person" expense depends on how many people are in your party. Solitary travelers can expect to spend somewhat more. Group expeditions may spend less per person on hotel rooms and taxi fares;

costs per person of restaurant meals and most public transportation will be the same no matter how many people are traveling together.

Excluding costs of air fares to and from Mexico, peso-pinching "Budget" travelers can do this 22-day trip for about US $500 (under $25 a day) per person. They'll take buses wherever possible and never rent a car or hire a taxi for day trips.

"Moderate" travelers should budget twice that amount, US $1,100 ($50 a day) per person, based on renting a car for the Caribbean Loop and renting taxis for several day trips.

The "Deluxe" traveler will rent cars for the entire trip and can expect to spend US $1,700 (about $80 a day).

Should You Rent a Car?
No question about it—a car is convenient, and most Americans are used to having at least one at their disposal. To rent a car in Mexico you must be over 24 years old, have a major credit card and a valid driver's license. Expect to pay at least $40 a day plus mileage for a standard size car. Most airports have several rental agencies. Shop around for a special.

Driving in Mexico is different than in the U.S. An experienced driver should encounter no major problems, but it's hardly relaxing. Driving in Mexico City is nightmarish—avoid it unless you've successfully tackled traffic in Tokyo or Rome or driven in demolition derbies. If you rent a car for the Colonial Loop, wait until you're ready to leave Mexico City to do so.

In Mexico, where fewer people own cars, public transportation is convenient, inexpensive and relatively comfortable. For sightseeing and getting around cities, it is actually cheaper to hire a taxi for a day than to rent a car.

Better yet, public transportation brings you into closer contact with the people, and the people are half the fun. Bus riding is "respectable" in Mexico. If you stick to first and second class buses (the difference is that first class has a bathroom aboard and stops less often) you won't be riding with pigs and goats. To experience *that* you'll need to take third class buses. Riding third class buses is a genuine adventure, but you'll never have to ride one on this 22-day itinerary unless you want to.

We recommend public transportation and taxis for the Colonial Loop and Oaxaca-Chiapas legs of your trip and renting a car for the Yucatán segment. The Yucatán can be done by bus and local day tours, but due to poorer bus service than in other parts of Mexico it's easier to drive. There's hardly a curve in the highways, traffic is light, there aren't many cities to drive through and the roads are well marked.

If you'll be driving a car on any part of this trip, be sure to read the information on driving in Mexico on pages 63-92 of *The People's Guide to Mexico* (see "Recommended Reading" below).

Hotels

As our old friend Carl Franz says, "Hotels are just places where you sleep, bathe and get some privacy." That you can do in any degree of simplicity or comfort you wish. In each town, we suggest hotels in three categories—Deluxe, Moderate and Budget. (Prices are about the same for a single or a double.)

Deluxe rooms will cost between US $19 and $25 unless otherwise specified. These hotels are *not* Hiltons or Sheratons (which, where they exist, are more expensive), nor are they the most expensive hotels in town. They do provide amenities and conveniences like in-hotel shops and travel agencies.

Moderate hotels cost US $10 to $18. The moderately priced rooms we've chosen are quite comfortable and, whenever possible, have a colonial flavor.

Budget hotels, with rates in the US $5 to $9 range, *are not* "bottom of the line." You'll have your own bathroom, and the rooms are clean.

Two important considerations in choosing your hotel room are temperature and noise. That upstairs room may have a view of the plaza, but the dedicated sleeper may prefer a darker and quieter interior room. In the Yucatán you'll want a fan or air conditioning; in the hill towns of the Colonial Loop and San Cristóbal, you may want an upstairs room (more heat from sunlight), or one with a fireplace.

Any hotel, however nice, may have its flaw. Once in Cancún we finally found a hotel that we could afford. We moved into our room and Tina blissfully flopped down on the bed. Her expression was not so blissful seconds later when she checked under the bedding and said, unbelieving, "This bed isn't a bed, it's just a box spring!"

Steve reported this shortcoming to the management. "What floor are you on?" the manager asked.

"The first floor."

"Oh," he said casually, "only the second floor rooms have mattresses."

We slept on the box spring.

When to Go

Mexico has two tourist seasons: winter and summer. Spring and fall are "off-seasons."

In the tropical lowlands, winter is the dry season and temperatures are generally moderate in most coastal areas. Expect temperatures in the 80s with clear days. In the Yucután the weather is similar except during *nortes* (wind and rain storms) that may last 3 or 4 days.

Winter in the highlands is also dry. It is generally warm and clear during the daytime. At higher elevations and in the north temperatures can drop below freezing at night.

Spring is the hottest time of year in the highlands, and it is windy. Expect hot, windy spring weather in coastal areas as well.

The rainy season starts in May and runs through October in most of Mexico. The highlands are often cool and sunny in the morning with cloudbursts in the afternoon. Coastal areas are hot and humid with frequent rain.

Fall is the hurricane season in the coastal areas. The highlands will be pleasant and green with lessening rain as winter approaches.

When NOT to Go

Mexico City just about empties out twice a year—during the Christmas season and Semana Santa (Holy Week, before Easter). If you find yourself on a beach you'll think the entire population of Mexico is there with you. Not only beaches but many smaller inland cities such as San Miguel de Allende and Oaxaca are popular spots for Mexican vacationers. To escape Semana Santa, we once traveled deep into the remote Lacandón jungle; even there, we were not alone! If you travel during one of these holiday times, you *must* make your airline and hotel reservations well in advance.

We always travel without hotel reservations the rest of the year. With a flexible attitude and a willingness to look around a little we've never found ourselves homeless for the night. Look over the list of fiestas in the back of this book while planning your trip. It's great to stumble upon a local fiesta, but without reservations there could be "no room at the inn."

What to Bring

Keep these items available in a day pack or shoulder bag:
Water purification drops. Three brands available in Mexican *farmacias* and supermarkets are Ni-bac, Elibac and Microdyn. If you only have access to tap water, use drops to purify it. Follow the instructions on the bottle. See how many *gotas* (drops) to use per *litro* (liter = slightly over 1 quart).
Toilet paper. Only bathrooms in the nicest restaurants have T.P.; public restrooms don't. The trick is always to carry a medium-size roll, instead of a big bulky one or a few shreds. If you figure out how to do this, please let us know!

Lomotil. Take one tiny tablet at the onset of *turista* (Montezuma's Revenge). Your doctor can prescribe it for you, or you can buy it without a prescription in Mexican *farmacias*. Use with moderation. You may never need Lomitil, but if you do you'll be glad you have it.

Earplugs. Mexico is *not* a quiet country. Most Mexicans don't even notice background noise, and often find too much silence *muy triste* (very sad). Earplugs, handy for catching a snooze on a bus or airplane, also let you turn down the volume on the typical nighttime medley of barking dogs and diesel buses and the early morning chorale of church bells, roosters and burros.

Small hand compass. It will help you follow maps and directions in this book. If you're driving, a compass will also help you navigate through cities.

Small flashlight. Great for exploring ruins and finding your way around darkened hotel rooms without awakening your travel companion. Many hotels don't provide reading lamps.

Mosquito repellant. Particularly necessary in the Yucatán.

Bandana. You can pick up a colorful cotton scarf at any Mexican market. Handy as a sweat rag or headband when exploring ruins, as a washcloth or bandage, and for 1,001 other uses.

Plastic water bottle. Gets you through long bus trips and that hot climb to the top of a pyramid.

Swiss Army knife. For peeling fruit and opening bottles along the road.

Hidden pocket or **money belt.** The best insurance against getting stranded without money in Mexico. For simple instructions to make your own, see Chapter 2 of Carl Franz' *The People's Guide to Mexico*. Inexpensive ($6) money belts can be ordered from Rick Steves' Back Door Travel, 120 4th Ave. N., Edmonds, WA 98020, (206)-771-8303.

What else to bring

As little as possible! Travel with one medium-sized piece of hand luggage and a day pack. If possible, start your trip with the suitcase half empty to leave room for that irresistible handmade ferris wheel and other folk art you'll collect along the way.

You'll also want to bring comfortable walking shoes. Tennies are fine; ten-pound hiking boots are overkill. Bring a warm sweater or jacket for the Colonial Loop hilltowns, or buy a beautiful wool sweater or poncho during your trip. Take quick-dry clothing that you can wash and dry overnight in your hotel room. Bring an adequate supply of film for your camera, since it's expensive in Mexico.

Recommended Reading

History & Archaeology
Many Mexicos, Lesly Byrd Simpson-History of Mexico.
Insurgent Mexico, John Reed-An American journalist's experiences in the Mexican Revolution.
Incidents of Travel in Central America, Chiapas and Yucatan (2 volumes) and *Incidents of Travel in Yucatan* (2 volumes), John Lloyd Stephens-Travels and adventures of one of the first archaeological explorers in the area.
People of the Serpent, Edward Thompson-Highly readable account of the experiences of the U.S. Consul to the Yucatan for forty years, starting in 1885.
If you want supplemental guidebooks to any of the ruins on your itinerary, the Museum of Anthropology in Mexico City has the best selection.

Culture and Sociology
Distant Neighbors, Alan Riding-In-depth explanation of Mexico's culture and political system, and the historical relationship between Mexico and the United States.
Five Families, Oscar Lewis-readable study of the Mexican family structure.

Fiction
Aztec, Gary Jennings-Historical novel of the Aztec empire before and during the Spanish Conquest; insights into pre-Columbian civilization with lots of gorey details.
The Power and the Glory, Graham Greene-Novel of a renegade priest forced underground during the Mexican Revolution.
The Bridge in the Jungle, B. Traven-Novel about the condition of Indians in Mexico through the first half of this century. We highly recommend this and any of Traven's other books on Mexico.

Travel Guides
The People's Guide to Mexico, Carl Franz-A MUST! And take it with you! This is *the* definitive "how-to" book of Mexican travel—by foot, car, plane, truck, bus, homemade RV, train, burro, kayak and dugout canoe. Carl Franz shows you how to handle just about every situation you may run into. Co-starring Steve!

Scheduling

To follow this itinerary like clockwork, please **arrive in Mexico City on a Friday**. The airline flights listed from Mexico City to Oaxaca and from Oaxaca to Tuxtla Gutiérrez are not daily flights, so if you modify this suggested itinerary you'll have to work out your own flight schedules.

Mexicans list departure and arrival times using the 24-hour clock ("military time"). Afternoon or p.m. hours are listed as 1300 through 2400. A 2:00 p.m. bus leaves at 1400 (*"catorce horas"*).

Nothing in Mexico moves *exactly* on schedule. One of the nicest things about Mexico is that it slows you down. People aren't in a hurry, and everything—from restaurants and bus schedules to public services—reflects that. As our friend Eve says, "Mexicans don't wait for the bus; they hang out, and when the bus comes along they get on it. In Mexico you learn how to 'not wait'."

Most stores or offices, including the post office, are closed from 2 to 4 p.m. or from 3 to 5 p.m. for *comida* (the main meal of the day) and *siesta*. To avoid endless frustration (a symptom of "schedule-itis"), get used to the big hole in the middle of the Mexican day. Many shops reopen until 7 or 8 p.m., making evening a good time for shopping. Most museums are closed on Mondays. You may discover other local idiosyncracies (for instance, in Pátzcuaro you can't buy liquor on weekends). Siesta is a good time to read, work on your travel journal, write postcards—or take a siesta yourself.

Documents

To get a tourist card (visa), you must show proof of citizenship—a passport, certified birth certificate, or notarized affidavit of citizenship. A vaccination certificate is not necessary. Your airline or travel agent can get your tourist card for you in advance, or you can pick one up at any Mexican consulate in the U.S. In any case you must get it stamped when you enter Mexico. Hang onto it—you'll be required to turn it in when you leave the country. A 30-day card is all you need for this trip, though you can get three- or six-month tourist cards.

Any child under 18 traveling to Mexico alone or with another person must have both parents' written, notarized consent. This means, for example, that a father traveling with his son must have the mother's notarized consent to the trip. The rule is not always enforced, but it may be.

Flying to Mexico
The cheapest way to fly to Mexico City from the west coast of
the United States is to go to San Diego, cross the border and take
a Mexican domestic airline flight (Aeromexico or Mexicana)
from Tijuana to Mexico City. Cheaper yet, buy the domestic
Mexican air ticket *in the U.S.* and avoid paying Mexico's 15%
IVA or value added tax. You can also catch a Mexicana
"tecolote" (owl flight) departing from San Francisco or Los
Angeles after midnight, and arriving in Mexico City between
5:30 and 8:30 a.m. *"Tecolote"* flights are quite reasonable. At
the time of this writing the San Francisco-Mexico City round
trip fare was $352, and the round trip fare out of L.A. was $235.
(Instead of flying, the budget traveler with time to spare can
catch a train from Mexicali to Mexico City via Mazatlan and
Guadalajara.)

From the midwest, the cheapest flights to Mexico City are
from Chicago on Mexicana Airlines. Midweek flights are
cheaper than weekends.

From the east coast, the best deal offered at the time of this
writing was an American Airlines round trip fare from New York
to Mexico City. It cost less than the conventional New York-
Miami, Miami-Mérida,Mérida-Mexico City route. Air fare
"deals" are changing constantly, so check what's current when
you're planning your trip. You can usually get lower rates by
buying your tickets a month in advance, and by accepting cer-
tain time limits on your return.

Airline schedules in Mexico are subject to change and should
be checked in advance.

Keep in Touch! While we work hard to keep the information
in this book up to date during the four to six months we spend
in Mexico each year, things change constantly. If this book
helps you enjoy a successful trip and you'd like to share your
discoveries, please send us your tips, recommendations,
criticisms and corrections c/o John Muir Publications, P.O. Box
613, Santa Fe, NM 87504. In return for recommendations used
we'll send you a free copy of our next edition.

"FE EN DIOS Y ADELANTE!"
(" Faith in God and Onward!")
[Slogan painted on a Mexican truck bumper]

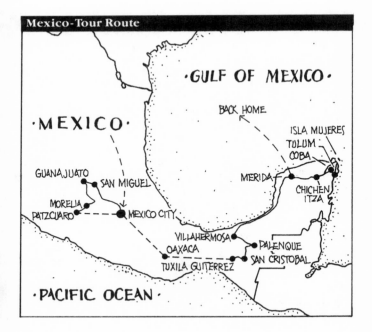

ITINERARY

We have to admit that without time limitations we'd probably spend six months taking this trip. Most of us, unfortunately, don't have that luxury but instead must fit our world travel into all-too-brief vacation time. If you only have three weeks (or less), this is an excellent itinerary for exploring a lot of Mexico and seeing where you'd like to spend more time later. For example, if the Chiapas jungle fascinates you, plan to explore the Usumacinta River on your next trip.

Colonial architecture, anthropology museums and Mexican art are fascinating—but so is a leisurely afternoon of people-watching in the town plaza or *tianguis* (market). While we've packed just about every hour of every day with sightseeing suggestions, don't hesitate to skip a few in favor of an unexpected adventure.

The three-week trip is divided into three segments. If your vacation time is limited, consider a one-week trip using the Colonial Loop, (Days 1-8) or the Yucatan segment (Days 17-22, starting and finishing in Mérida). For a two-week trip, go directly to Oaxaca via Mexico City and use Days 9 through 22. If you have more time—a month or more—add extra relaxation days to your itinerary or return to Mexico City on Day 22 and head straight for the Pacific beaches.

Here's an overview of the 22-day itinerary:

THE COLONIAL LOOP
Remember: Try to arrive in Mexico City on a Friday.

DAY 1   Arrive in Mexico City. Visit the airport tourist information office, get oriented, find your hotel and enjoy dinner.

DAY 2   Your first day in Mexico will be devoted to exploring the sights of Chapultepec Park. You'll visit the Museum of Anthropology, a splendid introduction to Mexico's culture and history. In the afternoon, tour Chapultepec Castle, once the elegant home of the Emperor Maximilian and his wife Carlota. Then see the Museum of Modern Art, the Rufino Tamayo art museum and/or the zoo. In the evening, if you're still energized, check out the nightlife in the Zona Rosa or Garibaldi Plaza.

DAY 3   This morning you'll take a walking tour of downtown Mexico City, including the Zócalo (main plaza), the National Palace's Diego Rivera murals depicting Mexico's history, and the Templo Mayor, recently discovered Aztec ruins. In the afternoon, tour the pre-Columbian ruins at Teotihuacán. Tonight, perhaps see the Ballet Folklórico.

DAY 4   Today you'll leave Mexico City by bus or rental car for
the colonial hilltown and artist community of San Miguel de
Allende. After lunch there will be time for people-watching,
window-shopping and a sunset walk.

DAY 5   Take a morning walk to visit more of the sights of San
Miguel. In the afternoon, bus or drive to the sanctuary at
Atotonilco, then relax in the hot springs at Las Grutas.

DAY 6   Leaving San Miguel early, travel to Guanajuato, the
beautifully preserved colonial state capital. Enjoy sightseeing
around town on foot, and watch the sunset from a scenic
overlook. After dinner, join in the evening fun on the main
plaza.

DAY 7   Today you'll travel from Guanajuato through Morelia,
Michoacán's state capital, to arrive at the Tarascan Indian town
of Pátzcuaro. Take a relaxed walk to see the sights.

DAY 8   After a morning in the Pátzcuaro market, take a boat to
the island of Janitzio for lunch. Late in the day you'll return to
Morelia to catch your plane back to Mexico City.

OAXACA TO PALENQUE
DAY 9   Arriving in Oaxaca, visit the Tianguis (Indian market),
where you can buy excellent weaving and folk art from colorfully dressed Indians. Take an afternoon walk to see museums
and churches. In the evening you may want to watch folk
dancers performing at a downtown hotel.

DAY 10   Tour the outlying areas of Oaxaca, visiting the Sunday market in Tlacolula and ancient ruins including Mitla and
Yagul. On the way back to the city you'll have a chance to visit
the village of Teotitlán del Valle and watch some of Mexico's
finest weavers at work. After dinner, join the Sunday evening
promenade on the downtown plaza with its bandstand and
lovely jacaranda trees.

DAY 11   Exploring the spectacular Zapotec ruins of Monte
Albán will be today's highlight. You'll also have time for more
marketplace browsing and shopping.

DAY 12   A day of hard traveling: fly from Oaxaca to Tuxtla
Gutiérrez, then proceed by bus to the highland Maya town of

San Cristóbal de las Casas, the most Guatemala-like town in Mexico. Check into your hotel and rest.

DAY 13   Explore San Cristóbal on foot. Later in the afternoon, visit Casa Na-Bolom, the residence and museum of renowned anthropologists, Gertrude Duby and the late Frans Blom.

DAY 14   This morning you'll travel from San Cristóbal to Palenque. After checking into your hotel and making tour reservations for tomorrow, you'll have ample time to cool off in the swimming pool and look around town.

DAY 15   Explore the Mayan ruins of Palenque, a quintessential "lost city" in the jungle. Later in the day you can taxi to the magnificent waterfalls of Agua Azul.

DAY 16   After a relaxing morning in Palenque, you'll take the bus to Villahermosa to catch your flight to Mérida, your home base in the Yucatán.

THE YUCATAN
DAY 17   Today is for sightseeing around Mérida, exploring the Museum of Anthropology, visiting the zoo and mingling with Maya Indians in the marketplace. In the evening, after feasting on fabulous Mayan cuisine, watch Mérida's Ballet Folklórico.

DAY 18   Leaving Mérida at dawn's early light, you'll arrive on Isla Mujeres around sundown. On the way, explore the great Maya/Toltec ruins of Chichén Itzá.

DAY 19   Isla Mujeres is a beautiful tropical island with fine beaches. Enjoy!

DAY 20   Go snorkeling at El Garrafón, the beautiful underwater National Park, and see the sea turtles, visiting the Mayan temple at Ixchel for sunset. Or spend another day sunning yourself on the beach.

DAY 21   Returning by ferry to the mainland, spend a couple of hours at the wildlife sanctuary lagoons of Xel-Ha, then visit the magical seaside Mayan ruins at Tulum, ending up at your end-of-the-trip "splurge" hotel near Cobá.

DAY 22   After investigating Cobá, the least-explored and least-reconstructed ruin on your itinerary, you'll return to Mérida for your last dinner in Mexico and rest up for your trip home the next day.

DAY 1
ARRIVE IN MEXICO CITY

Arrival Checklist
■ After claiming your baggage, exchange U.S. dollars for pesos at the bank in the airport.
■ Go to the Tourist Information booth in Section A of the airport for maps, a hotel reservation if you need one, and information on taxi tickets.
■ Make your Mexico City hotel reservation for Day 8.
■ Make your airline reservations for Morelia-Mexico City (unless you're renting a car for the Colonial Loop) and Mexico City-Oaxaca.
■ Buy taxi ticket. Take taxi to your hotel and get settled there.
■ Have your hotel make reservations for the Ballet Folklórico Sunday night. (Or you can buy them on your downtown walk tomorrow.)
■ Have dinner in your hotel and get a good rest.

Airport Orientation
The airport banks are open longer hours than the downtown banks and often give a slightly better exchange rate. Most large hotels will accept dollars or travelers checks, but usually at a lower exchange rate. You can only exchange money at a bank between the hours of 10:00 a.m. and 1:00 p.m. and it may mean standing in long lines, so we suggest changing enough money to cover your estimated expenses for a week at a time. Try to change enough to get through the following Monday, the busiest day at banks.

The Tourist Information Center will help you make your hotel reservation at no charge. While you're there, get maps of the city and the Metro. Buy a taxi ticket to your hotel, sold at both ends of the terminal. Taxi tickets protect you from being overcharged by voracious cabbies. It's at least a 30-minute trip from the airport to the city center.

Tourist Information recommends three hotels convenient to the airport, and you'll want to make reservations at one of them for Day 8 of your tour, seven days from today. The **Fiesta Americana** (tel. 762-0199) and the **Holiday Inn** (tel. 762-4088), both on Blvd. Aeropuerto, are expensive by Mexican standards— about US $50 single or double. If you don't want to spend that much, book a room at **El Reazor** (Viaducto Miguel Aleman #297, tel. 657-3062 or 652-4470)—about US $17 for a double, and only 7 or 8 minutes from the airport.

Now's the time to buy your airline tickets for later in the

itinerary. Unless you're planning to rent a car for the Colonial Circle portion of your tour (Days 4 through 7), get tickets for Aeromexico Flight #143 from Morelia to Mexico City at 5:25 p.m. on Day 8. (Budget travelers may want to substitute a bus ride.) Everyone will need tickets from Mexico City to Oaxaca on Mexicana Flight #201 at 9:40 a.m. on Day 9.

Mexico City Orientation

Welcome to "The Big Enchilada"!

When Cortés first arrived in Mexico City (then called Tenochtitlán) in 1519, it was already larger than any European capital city. It still is. In fact, this awesome megalopolis, whose population is variously estimated at from 18 million to 21 million, is probably the world's largest city. Amazingly, however, the overcrowded populace is usually helpful and friendly.

Mexicans call the capital city simply "México" or "D.F." (pronounced "day-effay," which stands for *distrito federal*). Its official name, Mexico, D.F., is equivalent to our Washington, D.C.

Mexico City is located 7,500 feet above sea level in a high valley surrounded by mountains. This valley, formally known as the Valley of Anáhuac, was once covered with forests and lakes. The climate is temperate with the temperature hardly ever going below freezing and rarely getting really hot. The rainy season is between the months of May and October, but it occasionally rains at other times as well.

According to legend the Aztecs came to the Valley of Mexico in 1325 and founded the city of Tenochtitlán on an island where they saw an eagle sitting on a nopal cactus with a snake in its beak, as foretold by prophecy. The Aztecs dominated the region and the city grew to an estimated 500,000.

The Spaniards under the leadership of Hernan Cortés arrived in 1519. The Aztecs thought Cortés was the god Quetzalcoátl (the Plumed Serpent—you'll be hearing a lot about him) returning as prophesied. Quetzalcoátl was reputed to be light-complected with a beard, so Cortés and his men fit the description. That made it much easier for the small force of around 500 Spaniards, backed up by tens of thousands of Indians who loathed the Aztecs, to beseige the city of Tenochtitlán, capture its leaders and virtually destroy the city in the process. The conquistadores enslaved the Indians and started rebuilding the city in European style. They built great cathedrals and palaces with much of the building material coming from the razed Aztec temples and buildings.

The city grew slowly over the years and the lake eventually dried up. By 1930 the population of the city was only one million. Incredible growth has taken place in the last fifty years, bringing about destruction of the valley's environment as the city's cars, buses and factories spew out a world-class smog.

We'll be confining our explorations to only a few areas of this endless urban sprawl: the central historical downtown area, Chapultepec Park and the Zona Rosa, and the pyramids of Teotihuacán, an hour's drive north of the city.

Transportation in Mexico City

Mexico City's intricate bus system will get you to any part of the city, however obscure. But you'll find it much simpler to rely on the Metro (subway), *peseros* (shared taxi vans) and taxi cabs.

The Metro: Mexico City's subway has recently had a 2,000% fare increase! It used to cost one peso to ride; now it costs twenty pesos (less than US 4 cents) to ride anywhere in the city— still the world's best transportation bargain. The Metro is surprisingly clean, quick and comprehensive. Subway tickets are sold five at a time. There are presently seven subway lines, with more under construction. Each line is identified by a color and by the names of the two stations at the ends of the line.

Getting around by Metro is easy if you know where you are and where you're going. To get started in the right direction, identify the name of the terminal station in the direction you want to go. For example, if you're going to the Zócalo on Line #2 from your hotel near the "Revolución" station, you will be traveling in the direction of "Tasqueñá."

The map shows the stations for transferring from one line to another. To change lines, follow the signs that say "Correspondencia" and the name of the terminal station in the direction you're going. Some connections are quite simple; other times, you'll find yourself walking for what seems like miles through underground passages, following arrows up and down escalators and across ramps.

Suitcases, backpacks and large bundles are not allowed on the subway, though you may be able to get away with it outside of rush hours.

Cautionary note: The Grope. Like subways the world over, the Big Enchilada's Metro system has its share of creeps with "the feelies." Tina carries a large shoulderbag on a long strap, which can be wedged between herself and a likely "groper." She also doesn't hesitate to turn and jam a fist into an offender's belly, stamp sharply on his foot or say loudly *"¡Quítate tus manos!"* ("Keep your hands to yourself!") The timid may prefer to take a cab.

Several friends have been pickpocketed on the Metro. Be sure to carry any valuables in your hidden pocket or money belt.

Mexico City Metro (subway)

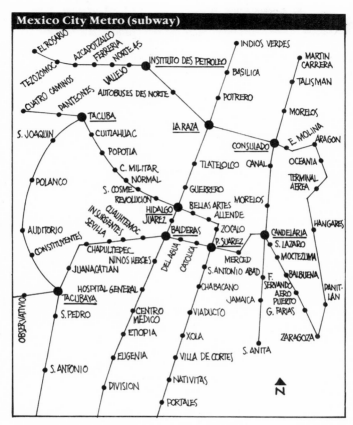

Avoid rush hour subway travel (7:00-10:00 a.m. and 4:00-7:00 p.m.) at all costs!

Useful Metro vocabulary: *Salida* = Exit. *Andenes* = Boarding platforms.

Peseros: As you might deduce from the name, *peseros* (shared taxis, also called *colectivos* or *combis*) used to charge a single peso for a ride. Nowadays, the first kilometer in a pesero costs 70 pesos, with an additional charge for longer distances. A network of these green and white Volkswagen mini-buses covers the entire city. You'll mostly use those that run up and down Paseo de la Reforma. To flag one down, step off the curb into the life-threatening traffic and wave.

Accommodations

For a deluxe downtown choice, we recommend the **Hotel Majestic** (Madero #73, tel. 521-8600). Its handsome tiled lobby with fountain is inviting, and the 6th floor rooms with small balconies offer the best view of the Zócalo.

Our favorite moderately priced hotel in all of Mexico City is just a ten-minute walk from the Zócalo, right on Plaza Garibaldi, the heart of mariachi music in Mexico. The **Hotel Galícia** (Honduras #11, tel. 529-7791) has attractive and comfortable rooms with color TV, a perfect retreat from the authentic Mexican musical madness on the plaza. Ask for a quiet room.

The best budget hotel we've found, just a block and a half from the Zócalo, is the **Hotel Canadá** (Avenida 5 de Mayo #47, tel. 518-2106), where you can get a clean, adequate double for about US $10.

The Zona Rosa, on the south side of Paseo de la Reforma near the Monument to Independence ("the Angel"), is a popular international tourist area noted for exclusive and fashionable shops, restaurants and clubs. If you have the urge to spend more money than you need to, the **Hotel Calinda-Geneve** (Londres #130, tel. 211-0071) provides the insulation and security of three restaurants, as well as its own travel agency and bookstore. The rooms aren't really any better than those at the moderately-priced **Del Angel**, just across the Reforma at **Río** Lerma #154 (tel. 533-1032). Down the street at Río Lerma #31 is the charming **Hotel María Cristina** (tel. 546-9880). For a budget hotel close to the Zona Rosa, you can't beat the **Hotel María Angelo's** (Río Lerma #11, tel. 546-6705). Their US $8 doubles are clean, though threadbare, and even come with a tub—a *norteamericano* luxury rarely encountered on the budget hotel circuit.

For an oxygen-rich atmosphere of greenery and quiet, try the **Hotel Polanco** (Edgar Allen Poe #8, tel. 520-6040) near Chapultepec Park. To avoid noise, be sure to ask for a room *"que no está cerca de la bomba"* ("which isn't near the pump"). The Polanco is right next door to the Restaurant Parador de Manolo, specializing in truly excellent Spanish cuisine at moderate prices.

Which brings us to Steve's favorite subject . . .

Food

You could spend your whole vacation sampling the international cuisine of Mexico City. Thousands of restaurants range
from quick-and-simple *loncherías* to those offering full
gourmet dinners. Much as Steve would like to, we haven't been
able to sample them all; but after prolonged eating, here are
some of our favorites. All are moderate to inexpensive.

When in the Zócalo area, have lunch at **Fonda Las Casuelas**,
República de Colombia #69. Don't let the run-down neighbor-
hood scare you off. This beautifully decorated restaurant serves
excellent Mexican specialties. Try the tortilla soup for a real
treat.

The **Hosteria de Santo Domingo** (Belisario Dominguez
#72, just off Republica de Chile) is reputed to be the oldest
restaurant in the city. They serve traditional Mexican food, the
service is great and the prices are the most reasonable anywhere for a restaurant of this class. If you are in luck, there may
be two old gentlemen playing Scott Joplin on piano and violin.
Feeling adventurous? Try the chiles en nogada, a chile relleno
variation stuffed with meat and walnuts in a creamy sauce
decorated with pomegranate. Another old-time downtown
restaurant is the **Café Tacuba** (Tacuba #28). The typical Mexican food is unexceptional, but it's worth a visit for the atmosphere. You might also try the Sunday lunch buffet at the Hotel
Majestic for a great view of the Zócalo and lots of food *estilo
ranchero* (country style). Enjoy mariachi music while you eat.

El Danúbio (Uruguay #3) is a very good seafood restaurant
with a huge afternoon comida corrida. Steve has been making
pilgrimages there since 1959, and the huachinango veracruzano
(red snapper in tomato sauce) has remained excellent. The
price, 10 pesos then, has changed, but the waiters are the same,
only older. A cab driver guided us to another good seafood
place, **Los Jarochos** (Calle Honduras #17-1, just down from
Plaza Garibaldi). The sopa marinera (sailor's soup) is excellent
but not for the fainthearted as it contains octopus, sardines and
all manner of other sea life; served only on weekends.

The huge "eating market" right off Plaza Garibaldi contains
many fondas—small market stall restaurants serving dishes
such as bírria (pit barbecued goat in a juicy sauce), pozole (pork
and hominy soup) and carnitas (delicious pork served with tortillas and salsa). Competition is fierce and each stall has its
barker trying to lure you in. A whole meal costs about US $1
and is a memorable experience.

The Zona Rosa is packed with restaurants—Japanese,
Chinese, French, Spanish, Italian, German and, yes, Mexican . .
you name it and you'll probably find it. Even the expensive

ones won't cost you much more than a pig-out at a U.S. Burger King. Stroll down Calle Copenhague between Hamburgo and Paseo de la Reforma and you'll find an assortment of sidewalk restaurants. We particularly like **Mesón del Perro Andalúz** ("house of the Andalucian dog"), serving Spanish food. In the same block are the **Angus Steak House**, **El Perro d'Enfrente** (Italian), **El Chato** (Mexican), the **Picadilly Pub** and the **Verdi** (Mexican, international and pizza). For the bargain of a lifetime, try the "hole in the wall" **La Caretta Rosa** (Hamburgo #96). The lunch includes four courses, coffee and a cocktail, all for a little over US $1!

The restaurant downstairs at the Museum of Anthropology in Chapultepec Park offers better service and food than might be expected in a museum restaurant.

Check the *Mexico City Daily Bulletin*, available at most hotels. Explore on your own, and chances are you'll come up with other great finds.

A Word to the Wise
Like most big cities, Mexico City is notorious for thievery, some of it most ingenious. Our friend Deborah was visiting the Metropolitan Cathedral when suddenly she was spattered with what appeared to be bird droppings. A solicitous Mexican appeared at her side and guided her over to the baptismal font, indicating that she should set her purse down while she used the holy water to clean up. A second man made off with her purse, and her helpful "friend" energetically proclaimed his innocence.

Squirt guns full of bird poop?

Keep your wits about you and seek the Golden Mean between foolhardiness and paranoia.

DAY 2
EXPLORE MEXICO CITY

Today will be devoted to exploring the sights of Chapultepec
Park. *Chapultepec* is a Náhuatl Indian word meaning "Grass-
hopper Hill".

Suggested Schedule

8:00	Breakfast at hotel. Those who want to take a guided tour to Teotihuacán tomorrow should arrange it through your hotel now.
9:00	Be at the Museum of Anthropology when it opens. Take an introductory tour and then explore at your leisure.
1:00	Lunch at the museum cafeteria.
1:30	Walk to Chapultepec Castle and take the tour.
3:00	Walk to the nearby Modern Art museum.
4:00	Cross the Reforma and see the Museo Rufino Tamayo. Or, if you're "museumed out," stroll in the Zoo or return to your hotel early.
5:30	Return to hotel.
7:00	Dinner. If you're still full of pep, check out the Zona Rosa or Garibaldi Plaza.

Sightseeing Highlights
▲▲▲**Museo Nacional de Antropología** (Museum of Anthropology)—Located on Paseo de la Reforma in Chapultepec Park,
this museum is reason enough by itself to visit Mexico City. The
handsome building houses 21 exhibition halls. The ground-
floor halls cover the origins of human life in Mesoamerica and
Mexico's ancient civilizations—Mexica (including Aztec),
Toltec, Oaxaca, Gulf Coast and Maya. The second-floor halls
show the cultures and lifestyles of the many indigenous groups
still living in Mexico today. Take a guided tour in English for a
nominal fee (just wait for five people to gather). It lasts about 45
minutes and covers the Aztec and Teotihuacán civilizations. Buy
a museum guidebook so you can locate those exhibits that interest you most. Panorama publishes a good one. Don't miss the
outdoor reproduction of the Bonampak murals and the magnificent panels from Palenque in the Maya hall, or the reproduction of Monte Albán Tomb 104 in the Oaxaca hall. If you want
supplemental guidebooks to any of the ruins on your itinerary,
this is the place to buy them. Museum hours: Tue.-Sat. 9:00
a.m.-7:00 p.m., Sun. 10:00 a.m.-6:00 p.m.

Chalpultepec

MUSEO NACIONAL DE ANTROPOLOGIA
MUSEO RUFINO TAMAYO
PASEO DE LA REFORMA
ZOOLOGICO
MUSEO DE ARTE MODERNO
MOLINO DEL REY
LAGO CHAPULTEPEC
GRAN AVENIDA
MONUMENTO A LOS NINOS HEROES
CHAPULTEPEC CASTLE
GRAN AVENIDA
CALZ. J. VASCONCELOS
CONSTITUYENTES
CALZ.

▲▲**Chapultepec Castle**—Built on the hilltop overlooking the park by the Viceroy Matias de Galvez in 1783, it later became a military academy. At the end of the Mexican War in 1847, six cadets died defending the castle from the U.S. Marines. The monument and massive pillars below commemorate these *Niños Héroes* (boy heroes).

The Emperor Maximilian and his wife Carlota lived here during their reign over Mexico. Walk around the terrace to the back of the building to see their restored furnished apartments. Be sure to see the Orozco mural in Sala 7. In the coach room, the coaches of Benito Juárez and Maximilian contrast the two leaders' lifestyles. You can take a 45-minute tour for US $1 per person, or a 1½-hour tour for US $2. Open Tue.-Sun. 9:00 a.m.-5:00 p.m.

▲▲▲**Museum of Modern Art**—Paseo de la Reforma and Calzada de Ghandi in Chapultepec Park. The museum has two buildings and outdoor sculpture gardens. The Galería building has temporary exhibitions, while the other building houses the permanent collection of works by contemporary Mexican artists. Open Tue.-Sun. 10:00 a.m.- 6:00 p.m.

▲▲▲**Museo Rufino Tamayo**—Paseo de la Reforma in Chapultepec Park. This museum was built to house the art collection of the great Oaxacan painter Tamayo. Exhibits include work by Picasso and other modern artists, as well as traveling exhibits. Open Tue.-Sun. 10:00 a.m.-6:00 p.m.

▲**Parque Zoológico** (the Zoo)—A must if you're traveling with children. See the Giant Condors and Panda. Open Tue.-Sun. 9:00 a.m.-7:00 p.m. Very crowded on Sundays, as are all Mexico City parks.

DAY 3
MEXICO CITY AND TEOTIHUACAN

This morning's walk will immerse you in the bustling life of downtown Mexico City. You'll spend the afternoon at the pre-Columbian pyramids of Teotihuacán, so mammoth that the Aztecs believed a race of giants had built them.

Suggested Schedule

8:00	Enthusiastic sightseers have an early breakfast and sneak in a visit to the Merced Market.
9:00	The rest of us get up and have breakfast.
10:00	Begin downtown walking tour with a stroll through Alameda Park.
12:30	Lunch downtown.
1:30	Trip to the Teotihuacan pyramids. Optional to stay for dinner at the museum restaurant and the 7:00 p.m. sound and light show.
6:00	Those who've had enough, return to Mexico City.
7:00	Dinner. Collapse into bed, or. . . .
9:00	Ballet Folklórico at the Bellas Artes.

Mercado Merced
This huge market, located in the center of old Mexico City, is easily reached by Metro. In fact, you can smell the vegetables of days gone by when you get off in the Merced subway station. If you love to eat, this is the most food you'll ever see under one roof! It's also a good chance to see the "nitty gritty" side of Mexico City. The nearby Mercado Sonora (take Avenida de Circumvalación to Fray Servando and make a left) has an awesome selection of ceramics, toys, miniatures, birds and witchcraft paraphenalia.

Downtown Walking Tour
Starting on the west end of Alameda Park, walk through the park to the domed Bellas Artes building. The Bellas Artes' exhibits include Diego Rivera's mural, "La Gran Victoria." Pick up your tickets for the Ballet Folklórico if you're planning to go tonight. Leaving Bellas Artes, make a left and then a right to the Museo Nacional de Arte, at Tacuba #8.

Afterwards walk back toward the Bellas Artes, take a left on Lázaro Cardénas, and notice the outrageous Post Office building. Turn left on Av. Madero and walk past the Casa de los Azulejos with its exterior of blue tiles, now a Sanborne's Restaurant. You will pass the Iglesia de San Francisco and the Iglesia de San Felipe de Jesús (*Iglesia* = church). In the next block on the right is the Palacio de Iturbide. Now a bank, its carved wooden doors are incredible. Peek in to see the wonderful stone pillared archways. You might want to browse the American Bookstore at Madero #25. In the fourth block you pass the Templo de la Profesa with its tower.

Arriving at the Zócalo, the Cathedral is on your left. Directly across from you is the Palacio Nacional (National Palace). The building on the far right houses offices of the Federal District. Go in and explore the impressive interior of the Cathedral. Next door is El Sagrario Metropolitano, originally the private chapel of the viceroy.

Enter the National Palace and make a left up the stairway. You'll be greeted by a gigantic mural of the Spanish conquest and the fight for independence. On the second floor a beautiful Diego Rivera mural shows Aztec life before Cortés. Outside again, nip into the Zócalo Metro station and see the models of the Zócalo at various stages of its history.

Leaving the Metro, head back toward the Sagrario. To the right you'll see a model of pre-Columbian Tenochtitlán. Walk through the ruins of the Templo Mayor. Time for lunch!

Sightseeing Highlights—Downtown Walking Tour

▲▲▲**Parque Alameda**—This beautiful park near the center of Mexico City was created at the beginning of the 17th century. During its first 200 years, it was on the edge of the city.

▲▲▲**Palacio de Bellas Artes** (Palace of Fine Arts)—Located at the east end of Alameda Park, this building is an extraordinary example of the late 19th century "art nouveau" style. Construction was interrupted by the revolution of 1910, and the theater was not completed until 1934. It is the home of the Ballet Folklórico and the National Symphony. To see the famous *cortina de cristales* (glass curtain) made of nearly a million pieces of stained glass and weighing 22 tons, you must attend a performance. The Bellas Artes museum has seven exhibition halls including murals by Rivera, Tamayo, Siqueiros and González Camereva. Open Tue.-Sun. 10:00 a.m.-6:30 p.m.

▲▲▲**Museo Nacional de Arte**—Tacuba #8, across from the *Correo* (Post Office). The paintings by José María Velasco (1840-1912) are a fascinating record of the beautiful Valle de México as it was before the city ate it up. Notice how much of the great lake existed as late as the last century. Open Tue.- Sun. 10:00 a.m.-6:00 p.m.

▲**Casa de los Azulejos** (House of Tiles)—Calle Madero #4. Built by the counts of the Valley of Orizaba, the interior with its tile-covered staircase and beautiful patio is now a popular restaurant and shops.

▲▲▲**Plaza de la Constitución** (*El Zócalo*)—The central plaza of Mexico City came to be called the Zócalo because a huge base for a statue (*zocalo*) was built here in 1843, though the statue itself was never completed. The word zócalo has come to mean central plaza throughout Mexico.

▲▲▲**Catedral Metropolitana**—The largest religious building in the Americas, this magnificent cathedral was begun in 1567 and finished in 1813. Inside are five huge altars, fourteen side chapels and a black Christ known as *El Señor del Veneno*— The Lord of the Poison.

▲▲▲**Palacio Nacional**—The National Palace was built in the 16th century on the site of Moctezuma's palace. It was the viceroy's residence in colonial times, and now houses the executive branch of the Mexican government, spectacular murals by Diego Rivera and a couple of dull museums. Mexico's liberty bell adorns the central balcony.

▲**Plaza de Garibaldi**—Lazaro Cardenas at Honduras street, about a ten-minute walk north from the Palacio Nacional. Mariachi bands gather here in the evening to play in the plaza or in nearby nightclubs. Besides Mariachi bands (the ones with trumpets, violins and the huge bass guitar called *guitarón*) you'll hear Norteño bands with accordian, and Jarocho bands from Veracruz with huge harps. Motorists stop their cars along the main street passing the plaza for a few quick songs at the "drive-in serenade." The Bar Tenampa on this plaza serves a famous ponche de grenada (pomegranate punch).

▲▲▲**Templo Mayor**—Ceremonial heart of the Aztec capital of Tenochtitlán, a pyramid over 150 feet high was destroyed by the conquistadores. On top of the pyramid were two temples dedicated to the gods Huitzilopochtli (war god) and Tlaloc (rain god). This ruin was discovered in 1978 by workers burying an underground cable. The famous Aztec Calendar Stone was found nearby in 1790.

The Pyramids of Teotihuacán

Teotihuacán is a Nahuatl Indian name meaning "the place where gods were created." This site dates back to 150 B.C., when the substructures of the Pyramids of the Sun and the Moon were built. According to legend, the fourth sun burned out before man existed. The gods gathered at Teotihuacán and decided that one of them should be sacrificed and turned into a Sun. Two of the gods leapt into the sacrificial flames and were transformed into the Sun and the Moon. It is estimated that the city of Teotihuacán flourished from about 100 B.C. to 700 A.D. The central axis of the ceremonial city runs north-south and was named The Avenue of the Dead by the Aztecs, based on their mistaken belief that the large mounds on either side were graves.

Getting there

Teotihuacán is located 32 miles north of Mexico City. Innumerable tours are available to the pyramids, ranging in price from US $6 up. Most leave in the morning, so you may wish to rearrange your schedule and do your downtown walk in late afternoon. Check with your hotel for tour information. Some pyramid tours include a visit to the famed Basílica de Guadalupe.

Getting to Teotihuacán by bus on your own is fairly simple. Take the Metro to station "T.A. Norte" (for *Terminal de Autobuses Norte*). Once in the bus station, find the bus line called "México San Juan Teotihuacán Otumba Apam Capulalpan y Ramales, S.A. de C.V." The key word is Teotihuacán, and you'll find the ticket office near the big green and white sign that says "Espera #8" (Waiting Room #8). Buses leave every half-hour from 7:00 a.m. to 3:00 p.m. The trip takes about an hour. Don't miss the last bus back at 6:00 p.m. The bus drops you off on the highway at the cobbled driveway leading to the museum entrance, and picks up returning passengers at the same spot.

Teotihuacán

TO MEXICO CITY

TICKETS

UNDERGROUND BLDGS,
PALACE OF THE JAGUARS

PYRAMID OF THE MOON

PARKING

MUSEUM   PARKING

PALACE OF
THE PLUMED BUTTERFLY

STREET OF THE DEAD

PYRAMID OF THE
SUN

TEMPLE OF
QUETZALCOATL

THE CITADEL

SUN PALACE

PLAZA OF THE MOON

PARKING

N

TEPANTITLA

Walk through the Ruins

Start at the **Museum**, with its reproduction of the water goddess Chalchiuhtlicue (the first of a long series of Aztec and
Mayan tongue-twisters). See the wall paintings collected from
various temples.

Directly opposite the museum is **The Citadel** (*La Ciudadela*).
Excavation revealed that this superstructure covers an older,
much more impressive and ornate monument, **The Temple of
Quetzalcóatl**, now partially revealed at the rear of the complex. Built between 200 and 250 A.D., this pyramid is adorned
with sculptured heads of the feathered serpent Quetzalcóatl
and another more stylized figure, identified as either the rain
god Tlaloc or the corn god. Take your pick. Carved stone
seashells are interspersed in the coils of Quetzalcóatl's body.

Returning to the main avenue, walk north through a series of
large stepped patios toward the Pyramid of the Moon. In the
first patio on the left metal roofs cover the excavated **Underground Buildings**, which you can walk through. They
weren't originally underground, of course, but were buried in
the MesoAmerican practice of building new monuments over
old ones, gradually raising the ground level.

Patios 2-5 are unexceptional, though the second patio has a
floor of sheet mica (the **Viking** or **Mica Floor Complex**) hidden by the thick floor of cement and stucco. The last of the
stepped patios brings you to the **Plaza and Pyramid of the
Sun**. The pyramid's base is comparable in dimensions to the

Great Pyramid of Egypt, though barely half as tall. The height difference will seem negligible if you decide to huff it to the top. The Spaniards destroyed a stone idol measuring "three fathoms" (eighteen feet) that topped this temple. **The Palace of the Sun** lies in front of and slightly north of the pyramid.

Continuing north toward the Pyramid of the Moon, you will see a shed roof on the right which protects the remains of a mural painting of a jaguar. When you get to the **Plaza of the Moon**, make a sharp left at the corner and go up the steps of the **Palace of the Plumed Butterfly** (Quetzalpapalotl). At the top of the stairway, on the north side (in front of the pillared hall containing the remains of murals in red) is a huge serpent's head. The inner courtyard has pillars adorned with the mythological butterfly that gives this palace its endearing name. Some decorative obsidian disks remain in the bas-reliefs.

Retracing your steps, leave the palace and turn right. A narrow stairway terminates in a large courtyard, the **Palace of the Jaguars**. Built in 450-650 AD, this building features murals of a jaguar either blowing into or drinking out of a feathered conch. As you exit this courtyard, a modern tunnel to the right leads you into the **Substructure of the Feathered Shells** built in the second and third centuries A.D. Located under the Quetzal-butterfly's palace, this temple is adorned with bas-relief sculptures of feathered conches with mouthpieces, presumed to have been musical instruments, and four-petaled flowers. A low platform decorated with murals of green birds, best seen on the way out on the southeast side, supports the temple.

Leaving this complex of buildings, return to the Plaza of the Moon and gird yourself for another *subida y bajada* (ascent and descent). **The Pyramid of the Moon**, composed of four huge sloping terraces, ends our walk up this grand road.

But you're not through yet! If you've got it in you, it's worth a side trip on your way back to see **Tepantitla**, with its remains of the mural of the **Paradise of Tlaloc**, depicting human figures at play, chasing butterflies and bathing. To get there, hook a left just north of the Pyramid of the Sun. Walk through Parking Lot #2 and down the road linking it to Tepantitla, about half a mile from the main avenue. (Out of energy? You can see a reproduction of the mural in the museum.)

It takes three hours at a brisk trot to see the Teotihuacán ruins. Add 45 minutes for each pyramid climb. Of course, you may want to linger longer, or take a few minutes to buy a dozen clay whistles and a couple of crystal balls. (Vendors swarm here like mosquitoes.)

DAY 4
SAN MIGUEL DE ALLENDE

Today you'll leave Mexico City for the beautiful old hill town of
San Miguel de Allende, the adopted home of many foreign artists and expatriates. You'll spend the afternoon enjoying the
shops, parks and narrow cobbled streets of this colonial town.

Suggested Schedule	
9:00 a.m.	Leave Mexico City.
1:00 p.m.	Arrive in San Miguel de Allende, get settled in your hotel and have lunch.
3:00 p.m.	Sit in the plaza, locally known as the *jardín* (garden), and people-watch. Slip into the Parroquia and San Rafael churches.
4:00 p.m.	Check out some of the craft shops and boutiques.
5:00 p.m.	Walking Tour #1
7:00 p.m.	Dinner. Afterwards, sample San Miguel's nightlife.

**Transportation: Mexico City—San Miguel de Allende
(180 miles)**
By car: If you rent a car in Mexico City for this part of the trip,
do so at the airport. There is a large selection of rental agencies
in the airport and you'll avoid driving in downtown Mexico City.
You'll leave the city on freeways and connect with toll road
#57-D toward Querétaro. Ask at the airport tourist information
booth for directions to the car rental area. The rental agency
will provide maps and highway directions to Querétaro. When
you reach Querétaro, follow the signs for San Luis Potosí to
bypass the city. About half an hour past Querétaro a sign marks
the turnoff to San Miguel de Allende on the left.
By Bus: Take a taxi to the Terminal del Norte bus station. Two
first-class lines serve San Miguel: Tres Estrellas de Oro and Om-
nibus de Mexico. Second-class lines are Flecha Amarilla and
Herradura de Plata. Find the ticket office for one of these bus
lines and buy your ticket. Service is frequent, so one of them
should have a bus just ready to leave. The trip takes about 4
hours.

Orientation—San Miguel de Allende
In the mid 16th century San Miguel was a Spanish military out-
post and the site of a mission founded by Fray Juan de San

Miguel. It was incorporated as a town in 1555, and took its present name, San Miguel de Allende, from the revolutionary hero born here.

Once a compact colonial hill town, San Miguel is fast sprawling in all directions. Fortunately, the Mexican government has preserved the timeless charm of the city center by declaring it a national historic monument.

San Miguel's two art schools, the Instituto Allende and Bellas Artes, have attracted foreign students for the past forty years, and many have stayed. To see why, wander around and discover handsome colonial facades, a balcony wild with geraniums or your own favorite crooked little alley.

The state of Guanajuato has been a rich mining area since colonial times, producing great quantities of silver, opal, fire agate, amethyst and other gemstones. Silverwork and high quality jewelry can be found in the shops of San Miguel. There is also metalwork in brass and tin, including elaborate and ornate mirror frames, glass boxes, lampshades, etc. There is textile work in wool and cotton, and in San Miguel you can buy heavy wool sweaters and jackets knitted by jail inmates. The handsome and fanciful tiles produced in the town of Dolores Hidalgo, available in San Miguel, may tempt you to load up an extra suitcase to "do" your bathroom or kitchen.

Walking Tour #1

This one's for mountain goats, so if you're feeling lazy or creaky spend the time exploring shops, then take a cab to El Mirador just before sunset.

Follow Cuna Allende street (on the west side of the Parroquia), until it becomes Aldama and leads you right into Parque Benito Juárez, known locally as "French Park." Hopefully the lilies will be in bloom. Rest near a fountain or watch kids on the basketball courts.

Walk diagonally through the park and then up the hill to the left, past the public *pilas* where women wash clothes. Inhale deeply, then proceed up the steep zig-zag cobblestone walkway of El Chorro (the "spurt" or "stream," originally a public bathhouse.) Take the stairs to the front of the Capilla de la Santa Cruz del Chorro and continue ever upward on the cobbled alley to your right. Funky little Callejón del Chorro brings you to the road to Querétaro, just above El Mirador, a great spot for a panoramic photo.

San Miguel is dear to painters and photographers for its exquisite quality of light. After the spectacular *puesta del sol* (sunset) walk downhill and turn left into the second alleyway, Callejón de las Huertas. Continue downhill, turn right on

Recreo and follow your map to San Francisco Church. Then go on to the Oratorio de San Felipe Neri to see the ornate chapel of La Santa Casa de Loreto.

Sightseeing Highlights—Walking Tour #1

▲▲▲**La Parroquía** (the parish church)—The original simple church was built in the 17th century by architect Marcos Antonio Sobrarias. The ornate facade was added in the 1880s by mason Ceferino Gutiérrez who, so the story goes, copied a cathedral from a European postcard. This lovely building is in the center of town and its Gothic pink spires dominate the skyline.

▲**San Rafael**—The most notable feature of this simple church is a series of life-size dioramas depicting the crucifixion and scourging of Christ.

▲▲**San Francisco Church**—The churriguesque exterior contrasts with the serene and austere lines of the pink stone interior.

▲▲▲**Oratorio de San Felipe Neri** and **La Santa Casa de Loreto**—The marvelous towers and cupolas of this church add grace to San Miguel's skyline. The church houses the remarkable Santa Casa de Loreto, the original private chapel of the *condes* (colonial counts and titled personages). The chapel's floor and walls are covered in tiles from China, Valencia and Puebla. This is one of the most truly ornate chapels in Mexico, unique for its goldwork over carved stone rather than the traditional wood.

Accommodations

San Miguel has a great diversity of hotels and inns, with a wide range of prices.

For a splurge, **Hotel Posada La Ermita** (Calle Real de Querétaro #64, tel. 2-07-77) has spacious rooms with *salas* (sitting rooms) and balconies. This hotel is on a hilltop, with lots of stairs, and has a swimming pool. We like **Hotel Mansión del Bosque** (Alameda #65, tel. 2-02-72, write or call ahead for reservations)—charming, two meals included. **Hacienda de las Flores** (Hospicio #16, tel. 2-15-08) offers lovely modern accommodations behind an unprepossessing exterior. (These two hotels are a little more expensive than our "deluxe" price estimate.)

Moderately-priced bed & breakfast is available in the off-seasons (spring and fall) at **Posada Casa Carmen**, a pretty colonial hotel (Correo #31, tel. 20-84-4). In winter or summer you need reservations and lodging comes higher-priced with three meals daily. Other moderate hotels are the **Hotel San Francisco** right on the plaza (Plaza Principal #2, tel. 2-00-72), and **Posada de las Monjas** (Canal #37, tel. 2-01-71), a particularly good bargain.

Great budget hotels abound. Our favorite is the **Hotel Sebastián** (Mesones #7), which has big clean rooms, most with fireplaces—San Miguel can be chilly in the winter. The **Hotel Central** (Canal #19) is also a bargain. Or try the **Meson San Antonio** (Mesones #80).

Food

Aside from Mexico City, San Miguel is arguably the best eating town in Mexico. Thanks to the large foreign population and weekend migrations of *chilangos* (slightly impolite name for people from Mexico City), there are many specialty restaurants you wouldn't expect to find in a small Mexican town. Besides excellent Mexican cuisine you'll find everything from pizza to Chinese food.

Señor Plato (Calle de Jesús #7) has an international menu as well as Mexican specialties. Set in the patio of an elegant colonial mansion, it offers excellent service and food, full bar, Irish coffee, and a happy hour from 6:30 to 8:00 p.m. The restaurant-

bar **La Buganvilla** (Hidalgo #42) has been around San Miguel
for years in various locations. It serves well-prepared regional
dishes as well as an international menu. A newer establishment
with similar menu is **Restaurant La Casona** (#21 Canal) in the
Bazar Plaza Colonial. The service is particularly good here and
the food has always been good too; there's a bar. For diehard
carnivores lusting for an American-style steak we suggest the
Steak House Posada La Fuente (Calle Ancha de San Antonio
#95, near Instituto Allende). The menu consists almost entirely
of steaks (the best we've had in Mexico), served with tossed
salad and french fries.

For more economical eating, we like **La Casita** (Hernández
Macías #85), a pleasant place for lunch. Try the chicken soup!
Another good place for a full meal or a quick snack is the **Café
Colón** (San Francisco #21). The service is fast, the food is good
and the price is right. If you like chicken-fried steak, try the
milanesa at **Cenaduria El Retira**, Canal #25, our favorite San
Miguel "hole in the wall". It may well deserve the Best Milanesa
in Mexico Award.

For a real cup of coffee, espresso or capucchino, drop by the
Parroquiano-Casa de Té y Café (Insurgentes #74, across
from the public library). They have excellent desserts and
breakfasts, too. A good cup of coffee can also be found in the
folk art store **Pegasus** across the street from the post office on
Correos—they have a beautiful folk art collection, too.

San Miguel Nightlife

A popular and pleasant place to hear good music and perhaps
eat a late supper is **Mama Mia's** (Umarán #8, one-half block
down from the plaza). The music is usually better than the
food, but the pizza is quite acceptable and the service, though
slow, is friendly. With luck you may hear the excellent Spanish
flamenco music played by Wolf and Diana. At other times a
Mexican group plays Andean music as well as traditional Mexican music, salsa and rock (sometimes all at the same time!).

For everything from American country & western to jazz, try
the newly-opened **Pancho and Lefty's** (Mesones #99, closed
Mondays), serving drinks and light food. You can dance there
and sometimes things get pretty wild. San Miguel's expatriate
hangout, **La Fragua** (#3 Cuna de Allende) has a happy hour
from 6:00 to 8:00 p.m., with live music thereafter. Clifford
Irving often uses this bar as a setting in his novels. **La Princesa**
(on Recreo just up from the post office) features Mexican
popular music most nights and stays open late. Or for salsa and
jazz try **Corte Maltese** (Calle de Jesús #25, closed Wednesdays),
an Italian restaurant run by real Italians.

Helpful Hints

The local bilingual newspaper *Atención San Miguel* comes out on Thursday and is a good source of information on current art and music events. Available at the library, in supermarkets and at El Colibrí bookstore (southwest corner of the plaza, has books in English and art supplies).

We highly recommend María de la Cespede's Athanor Theater Company. Check in *Atención* for performance locations.

For additional information on San Miguel, visit the tourist office on the east side of the Parroquia near the Terraza restaurant. Open Mon.-Fri. 10:00 a.m.- 2:45 p.m. and 5:00-7:00 p.m., Sat. 10:00 a.m.-1:00 p.m., Sun. 10:00 a.m.-Noon.

The Biblioteca Pública (public library) at #25 Insurgentes has books, magazines and newspapers in English, and you're welcome to go in and read them. Open Mon.- Sat. 10:00 a.m.-2:00 p.m., 4:00-7:00 p.m.

DAY 5
SAN MIGUEL DE ALLENDE

Today you'll sightsee around town and then visit an unusual
penitent church. You'll then enjoy a delicious picnic lunch and
soak your weary bones in the hot springs of Las Grutas.

Suggested Schedule	
8:00	Breakfast.
9:00	Walking Tour #2.
1:00	Bus, taxi or drive to Atotonilco.
2:00	To Las Grutas. Soak, swim and picnic.
5:00	Return to town, relax before dinner.
6:00	Happy hour and dinner. Go out and listen to music or curl up in bed with a book.

Walking Tour #2
Walk down Calle Canal on the right-hand side where you have
a better view of the handsome Casa de Mayorazgo de Canal on
the northwest corner. Turn right on Hernández Macías and go
into the Bellas Artes. See the adjoining Iglesia de la Concepción.

(Detour: flea market buffs may want to check out the San
Miguel Tuesday Market. Follow Canal to the bottom of the hill,
and you'll see an outdoor market on your right.)

Continue down Canal and turn left onto Zacateros, which
takes you to Calle Ancha de San Antonio and the Instituto
Allende. Visit the galleries, then walk back to town on Hernández Macías to Cuadrante. Make a right to pass the Casa del
Carcél de la Inquisición on the corner. Turn left on Jesús and
follow your map back to the jardín. Go into the Casa de
Allende. Cross the square and go down Reloj. The building
decorated with gargoyles and Stars of David is the Casa Cohen.
Let the fragrance of the Blue Door Bakery seduce you into some
pan dulces (sweet rolls) for your picnic lunch.

Reloj will lead you to Insurgentes and, making a right, you
can walk up through the outdoor street market. Notice the
market's own shrine to the Virgin on the corner.

Stop in at the Iglesia de la Salud on Green Horse Square. (If
you don't see a green horse, it's because the statue was moved
to El Mirador for some mysterious reason. Locals still call this
the Green Horse Square anyway.) On the east side of the square,
make a left to get to the indoor market.

At a stand, have sandwiches made up for your picnic or,
if you prefer, pick up some *carnitas* (barbecued pork) sandwiches at Apollo #11 over on Mesones.

Sightseeing Highlights—Walking Tour #2
▲▲**Casa de Allende**—This former home of the revolutionary hero Ignacio de Allende has recently been restored and turned into a museum. It has not yet established a permanent collection but has rotating monthly exhibits. Open Tue.- Sat. 10:00 a.m.-5:00 p.m., Sun. 10:00 a.m.-3:00 p.m., closed Mon.

▲**El Tercer Orden**—The oldest church in San Miguel, built in 1713.

▲▲**Nuestra Senora de la Salud**—This simple church facade is capped by a large seashell design. Notice the collection of prayers, photos and *milagros* (lit. "miracles," small metal amulets) inside in front of the statue of the Niño de la Salud, evidence of healings, blessings and prayers answered.

▲▲▲**Iglesia de la Concepción**—The church was built between 1755 and 1765, and its cupola, designed by the same mason who did the Parroquia, was added in 1891. The interior of the church is of *cantera rosa* (rose-pink stone) and has a large gold-leafed altarpiece. Peek into the chapel behind the choir grille for a glimpse of the private chapel of the nunnery.

▲▲▲**Bellas Artes**—This art school is housed in the former Convent of the Church of the Concepción. Directly on the right as you enter is a bulletin board with announcements of current art exhibitions and concerts. There is a gallery on the left and a second gallery diagonally across the courtyard. In the little coffee shop attached to the second gallery you'll see the Pedro Martinez mural "La Pulquería" (""The Pulque Shop." Pulque is an alcoholic beverage made from the maguey plant). The galleries are open 10:00 a.m.-2:00 p.m. and 4:00-7:30 p.m. weekdays.

▲▲▲**Instituto Allende**—Founded in 1951, this art school occupies the former house of the Mayorazgo de la Canal. The history of the Instituto is on a display board in the entranceway. To the right is a bulletin board with a schedule of classes and notices of current events. There are two galleries: one displays works by painter James Pinto, the other rotating exhibits. To get to the galleries, make a left at the entrance and walk around the courtyard past the coffee shop and murals. Gallery hours are Mon.-Fri. 10:00 a.m.-1:00 p.m. and 3:00-6:00 p.m., Sat. 10:00 a.m.-Noon.

Atotonilco
A bus marked "Santuario" leaves on the hour from the southeast corner of Green Horse Square at the sign "Parada de Urbanos" (cleverly concealed by the "Farmacia San Miguel" sign). The half-hour trip costs about twenty cents.

The Sanctuary of Atotonilco and House of Spiritual Exercises was built between 1740 and 1802. Its interior is entirely covered with murals of angels and devils, flowers, leaves, fruits and mystical poems. Atotonilco attracts droves of pilgrims each year. Some penitents attempt to expiate their sins by wearing crowns of thorns and whipping themselves in imitation of Christ. Two weeks before Easter every year thousands of Mexicans walk in candlelit procession from the Sanctuary to San Miguel carrying the statue of Nuestro Señor de la Columna, arriving in the town at dawn.

Buses return to San Miguel every hour. Catch one heading back to town and get off at Manitiales de las Grutas.

Las Grutas

A number of natural hot springs around San Miguel have been developed as bathing spots. We find Las Grutas the most pleasant. Besides a big swimming pool, it offers a series of pools of graduated temperatures. The last and hottest pool is inside an artificial cave. During the summer all the lawns are green and you can eat bananas and figs from the plants overhanging the pools. Manantiales de las Grutas is open daily, 8:00-5:00, and costs about US $2 per person.

Flag down any bus on the highway to get a ride back to town.

DAY 6
GUANAJUATO

Today you'll leave San Miguel for Guanajuato. You'll have fun testing your wits against the underground streets and meandering alleyways of the city as you visit the sights. This is the place to cut loose and explore on your own.

Suggested Schedule	
8:00	Leave for Guanajuato.
9:30	Arrive in Guanajuato and check into a hotel. If you want a tour this afternoon, go to the tour office and sign up.
10:30	Begin Walking Tour #1 at the Basilica on Avenida Juárez.
1:00	Lunch.
2:00	Visit the market.
2:30	Walk #2, starting from the market.
3:30	Rént a cab at El Pípila for further sightseeing, or return downtown in time to catch your tour.
7:00	Dinner.
8:00	Drinks and people-watching on Jardín Unión.

Transportation
Catch a Flecha Amarilla ("Yellow Arrow") bus from San Miguel to Guanajuato at the bus station at the foot of the town about 8:00 a.m. Or you can leave town in style by taking a taxi from San Miguel to Guanajuato for US $15-20.

Drivers—Head out of town toward Celaya. Several miles out of town, make a right following the sign to Guanajuato. Once you get to Guanajuato you're on your own—there's no way we could possibly explain how to get around Guanajuato by car.

Orientation The elegant Jardín Unión in downtown Guanajuato belies the city's origins as a rough and ready mining town. Founded in 1557 to strip the earth of its incredibly rich silver deposits, the town grew along a canyon and up the sides of the surrounding hills. Some of the streets run underground through old mine tunnels and the former river bed, creating an incredibly complicated labyrinth. Its famous Granary Building is the site of one of the first battles in the Revolution for Independence from Spain. Shortly thereafter the Spaniards hung the heads of the leading insurgents on hooks at the four corners of the building, where they were displayed for ten years.

Guanajuato

TO DELORES HIDALGO

AVENIDA JUAREZ

TO MARFIL

PLAZUELA DE LOS ANGELES

- - - - SUBTERRANEAN STREETS

① JARDÍN UNIÓN ② TEATRO JUÁREZ ③ TEMPLO DE SAN DIEGO ④ PLAZUELA DEL BARATILLO ⑤ CORREO
⑥ TEMPLO DE LA COMPAÑÍA ⑦ UNIVERSIDAD DE GUANAJUATO
⑧ PLAZA DE LA PAZ ⑨ BASÍLICA DE NUESTRA SEÑORA DE GUANAJUATO
⑩ MUSEO DE PUEBLO DE GUANAJUATO ⑪ MUSEO DIEGO RIVERA
⑫ PLAZUELA DE SAN FERNANDO ⑬ PLAZUELA DE SAN ROQUE
⑭ PLAZA DE LA REFORMA (JARDIN MORELOS) ⑮ ALHÓNDIGA DE GRANADITAS ⑯ TOURIST OFFICE ⑰ BUS STATION ⑱ HOSPITAL
⑲ LAS MOMIAS (MUMMIES) ⑳ MERCADO HIDALGO ㉑ LA PURISIMA (BAKERY) ㉒ CALLEJON DEL BESO ㉓ EL PIPILA ㉔ IGLESIA Y MINA LA VALENCIANA ㉕ MUSEO DE MINAS ㉖ IGLESIA DE LA CATA ㉗ EX·HACIENDA DE SAN GABRIEL BARRERA

Guanajuato has a very European air, and in its many streets and alleys you would swear you had stepped into Italy. This is the ideal city to get lost in, and you probably will. Small alleyways and staircases open invitingly off the many intimate plazas, and the verb *callejonear* (to alley-walk) may well have been invented here. Whenever you find yourself lured off into unknown regions (lost!) just walk downhill and you'll find the centro again.

Guanajuato is famous (or infamous) for its mummies, which you may or may not wish to visit, and for its International Cervantino Festival in mid-October. People from all over the world attend the Festival plays and concerts. If you'll be there at Festival time, make hotel reservations six months in advance.

Accommodations

The most deluxe downtown hotel is the **Posada Santa Fe**, located on the jardín (Jardín Unión #12, tel. 2-00-84, 2-02-07); you usually need reservations one month in advance. Equally attractive is the **Hotel San Diego**, also on the square at Jardín Unión #1 (tel. 2-13-00).

Our favorite moderate hotel is the **Hacienda de Cobros**, near the bus station (Juárez #153, tel. 2-01-43). Our second choice is the **Mineral de Rayas** (Calle Alhóndiga #7, tel. 2-19-67).

For budget travelers we recommend the **Hotel Central** (Juárez #11, tel. 2-00-80) or the **Hotel Posada San Francisco** at the Plaza de Gavira, off Avenida Juárez near the market.

Food

The restaurant at the **Posada Santa Fé** has been written up in *Gourmet* magazine; it's a little expensive. The **Restaurant Valadez**, also on the jardín, has a moderately-priced and tasty comida corrida.

Steve highly recommends the **Tasca de los Santos**, a Spanish restaurant at Plaza de la Paz #28 across from the Basilica. There's good barbecued chicken at **La Carreta**, Juárez #96. Tina likes **El Claustro** on the Jardín Morelos, a good lunch stop after Walking Tour #1; you eat in the kitchen.

The **Bar Luna** has sidewalk tables on the jardín and good drinks. Try the Sangria, but watch out—it's stronger than it tastes.

Getting around

The main artery of the town is Avenida Juárez, which runs from the mummies past the market and basilica to the central plaza and beyond.

Tours: Transportes Turísticos de Guanajuato at Bajo Basílica #2

(on Avenida Juárez just below the basilica) has tours at 10:15 a.m. and 4:00 p.m.—if at least ten people are signed up. The tour bus will pick you up at your hotel if you make arrangements when you make your reservation. Tours are in Spanish unless you happen to get the one English-speaking driver. Steve calls this tour a totally Mexican experience, and very entertaining. The tour is supposed to last 3½ hours but may take as long as 5½ hours. Included are the mummies, El Pípila and a drive around the Panorámica, the village and church of Mineral de Cata and the Church of Valenciana. (Tel. 2-21-34 or 2-37-64.)
Taxis: If you prefer renting a cab to taking the tour, we suggest you include the ex-Hacienda de San Gabriel Barrera and the Mining Museum. You can negotiate a cab rental for US $3-5 per hour.

Walking Tour #1
Start walking at the Basílica on Avenida Juárez. Turn left out of the church and walk up Juárez to the Templo de San Diego on your right, facing onto the Jardín Unión, the central plaza. Visit Teatro Juárez right next door. Walk through this small elegant plaza to the Posada Santa Fé and turn right onto the mall leading out of the plaza.

Take the first left (in front of Pizza Piazza) into the Plazuela del Baratillo. Passing the fountain, follow the alleyway on the left to the Plaza de Compañía. This is a good time to buy stamps or mail letters at the *Correo* (post office) on the corner. Go into the Templo de la Compañía across the street. Continue on to view the unusual University building.

On the right just past the University is the Museo del Pueblo de Guanajuato. Continue on Pocitos until you come to the Casa de Diego Rivera.

After visiting this museum continue in the same direction, turning at the first left and an immediate second left that leads down to the Plazuela de San Fernando. The second exit on the right leads into the Plazuela de San Roque, equipped with bleachers and lighting for plays during the Cervantes festival.

Cross the plaza and go downstairs into Jardín Morelos (also known as the Plaza de la Reforma). Walk through the archway onto Juárez, turn right and then right again up the hill on Calle de Granaditas. The first left leads you to the Alhóndiga de Granaditas on the left.

Sightseeing Highlights—Walking Tour #1
▲▲▲Basílica de Nuestra Señora de Guanajuato—The 17th century baroque-style cathedral houses the 1,300-year-old statue, originally from Spain, of the Virgin Mary, patron saint of the city. The huge crystal chandelier over the altar is

locally known as *La Araña* (the spider). The church is located on the Plaza de Paz (Peace Square).

▲**Templo de San Diego**—The small churriguesque style church next to Teatro Juárez on the Jardín Unión dates from the 18th century.

▲▲▲**Teatro Juárez**—Completed in 1903 during the presidency of Porfirio Diáz, the beautiful Moorish theater's facade is embellished with Doric columns and statues. On the Jardín Unión.

▲▲▲**Templo de la Compañía**—This beautiful old church, built by the Jesuits, was completed in 1765. The elaborately carved churriguesque facade makes it the most spectacular of Guanajuato's 28 Catholic churches. (Aren't you glad you're only visiting five?)

▲**The University of Guanajuato** is considered one of the best universities in Mexico. The unusual school building looks old but was completed in 1955.

▲**Museo del Pueblo de Guanajuato** (Museum of the People of Guanajuato)—Located in the home of the Marques de San Juan Rayas, built in 1776, the museum has art exhibits, historical displays and murals by José Chávez Morado. Open Tue.-Sat. 10:00 a.m.-Noon and 4:00-7:00 p.m., Sun. 10:00 a.m.-4:00 p.m.

▲▲**Museo Diego Rivera**—The lower floor is a reconstruction of the home where Rivera lived until age six. Exhibits of some of his early work are on the upper two floors. Open Mon.-Sat. 10:00 a.m.-2:00 p.m., 4:00-7:00 p.m., Sun. 10:00 a.m.-4:00 p.m.

▲▲▲**Alhóndiga de Granaditas**—Completed in 1809 as the city grainery, this fortress-like building became famous as the place where the first battle for independence from Spain was won by insurgents Hidalgo, Ignacio Allende, Mariano Jiménez and Juan Aldama. Here El Pípilo, an Indian miner, set the door of the Alhóndiga on fire, allowing the insurgents to enter and rout the Spaniards holed up inside. Today the Alhóndiga is the Regional State Museum. There are many interesting exhibits of local history as well as an exhibition of arts and crafts from the state of Guanajuato. Open Tue.-Sat. 10:00 a.m.-2:00 p.m. and 4:00-7:00 p.m., Sun. 10:00 a.m.-4:00 p.m.

Walking Tour #2
This is a *subida* (hill climb). You may wish to take a cab ride instead to El Pípila and on to the itinerary suggested under "Getting around: Taxis."

Turn right as you leave the market and walk up Juárez to the Plazuela de Los Angeles. Take the first right on Callejón del Patrocinio, which is marked Callejonear Ruta #2. Take the first left on Callejón del Beso (so called because lovers leaning from one balcony to the other can kiss across the alley). Make a left,

following the Ruta #2 sign, at the next corner. Walk down to
Posada de los Angeles and make a right going uphill. At a rust-
red colored house with many pots of geraniums and ferns,
make a right. At this point you're going up Callejón de la Bar-
ranca. Just before the alley appears to dead-end in a private
home, there's a turn to the right—take it. Past the *tienda* (store),
make a left at the raised flower garden on your right, and continue up the obvious walkway to El Pípila.

Three gold stars if you made it without getting lost!

Sightseeing Highlights—Walking Tour #2 and Afternoon Tour

▲▲▲**Mercado Hidalgo**—This market, in a metal building that
looks like an old airplane hangar, features Day of the Dead candy (in shapes of skeletons) year-round. Food is downstairs,
artesanías (folk arts, handicrafts) upstairs.

▲**El Pípila**—Located on a *mirador* (overlook) on the Carretera
Panorámica, the big ugly statue of Juan José de los Reyes Martinez is better known as El Pípila. You came for the magnificent
view.

▲▲▲**La Iglesia de la Valenciana (Templo de San Cayetano)**
—Built in 1788. It is said that the Count of Valenciana, owner of
the nearby mine, required workers in the mine to contribute "a
handful of ore a week" toward the building of the church; then
he got the credit! The interior is graced with three huge altar
pieces elaborately carved and finished in 24k gold. The pulpit
of mahogany is inlaid with ivory and tortoise shell.

▲▲▲**La Valenciana Mine**—One of the richest mines in
history is now working again after being closed for years. It has
attractive park-like grounds and a shop where you can buy
silver jewelry. Take a look at the huge pit where ore is brought
up to be trucked to the smelter at La Cata. Beautiful quartz
crystals and other minerals are sold at shops in the nearby
village.

▲▲▲**Ex-Hacienda de San Gabriel Barrera**—This elegant
hacienda and extensive formal gardens adjacent to the Hotel
Presidente on the road to Marfil was a private home until First
Lady Mrs. Lopez Portillo donated it to the state in 1976. The
rooms are beautifully restored with their original furniture.

▲▲**El Museo de Minería** (Mining Museum)—A rockhound's
heaven! Two floors of glass cases filled with incredible crystals,
mineral specimens, fossils and cut gemstones. The museum is at
the Escuela de Minas y Metalurgia (School of Mines and
Metalurgy) on the road toward Dolores Hidalgo.

▲**Iglesia de la Cata**—Located at Mineral la Cata above the city.
Completed in 1725 and known as the miners' church, it has a

beautiful carved stone facade. Inside, the walls are covered with retablos—primitive drawings and descriptions of miracles answering prayers.

▲**Las Momias** (The Mummies)—A distasteful display of naturally mummified cadavers removed from the local cemetery because the rent on their graves was unpaid (the ultimate eviction). Some of the mummies have been on display for over 100 years. They are a popular tourist attraction. See them, if you must, at the *panteón* (cemetery).

DAY 7

GUANAJUATO—PATZCUARO

Today you will depart from Guanajuato, with its distinctly European flair, to enter a whole new world—that of the Tarascan Indians of Pátzcuaro. In the afternoon you'll take an easy walk around town to see some of the sights and absorb the atmosphere of this "laid-back" lake town.

Suggested Schedule

8:00	Earlybird departure from Guanajuato for Pátzcuaro by way of Morelia.
1:00	Lunch in Morelia on downtown plaza or near bus station.
2:00	Continue on to Pátzcuaro by bus or car.
3:00	Check into your hotel.
4:00	Take a gentle walk to visit the sights of Pátzcuaro.
6:00	Dinner. There isn't a whole lot to do here at night, so this is a good time to write some letters, catch up your journal or practice your Tai-Chi.

Transportation

Bus Riders: Back on the Yellow Arrow (Flecha Amarilla), the only bus line servicing Guanajuato-Morelia in the morning. Buses leave on the hour from 6:00 a.m. to 8:30 p.m. Catch the 8:00 a.m. bus. In Morelia, buses leave every half-hour for Pátzcuaro. You'll catch one after lunch in Morelia.

Drivers: Leaving Guanajuato, follow signs to Irapuato on Highway 45. Just before Irapuato, take the Querétero *quota* (toll road) to the Salamanca exit, Highway 110. Get in the right lane at the toll gate. Go into Salamanca and follow the signs to Morelia (Highway 43). After lunch in Morelia, just follow the signs to Pátzcuaro. There aren't very many; good luck!

Pátzcuaro- Orientation

In contrast to sophisticated San Miguel and cosmopolitan Guanajuato, Pátzcuaro is a slow-paced Tarascan Indian town. It's also flat, *gracias a Dios!* (Just as you were beginning to think all Mexican towns were built on the sides of cliffs. . .) The village which grew up on the shores of this lovely lake is famous for fishermen with butterfly nets.

The origin of the Tarascan Indian culture is unknown, but the Tarascan language, Purepecha, has linguistic similarities with both the Quechua spoken by Indians in Peru and the Japanese language. Tarascan legends, customs, music and religious rites resemble those of the ancient Incans in South America. Present-day Tarascans, or Purepechans as they call themselves, are an outgoing, friendly people who have kept many of their old traditions alive.

Pátzcuaro has two main plazas: the large and formal Plaza Don Vasco and the smaller Plaza Gertrudis Bocanegra, where the "action" is. This second plaza is the market center to which Indians from nearby villages bring their crafts. In the 16th century the Spanish bishop Don Vasco de Quiroga organized the region's villages so that each developed and perfected its own craft, preventing overproduction and competition between villages. As a result, this area is rich in copperwork, wood carving, textiles, straw work and pottery. Crudely carved wooden furniture as well as more ornate and sophisticated woodwork is for sale at roadside stands. In the Pátzcuaro market you will find carved wooden masks of many different styles, and colorfully painted wooden boxes and toys. Wooden musical instruments of varying quality are available in the town of Paracho, noted for its fine guitars.

Pátzcuaro

CORREO · BUS STATION · BIBLIOTECA PÚBLICA · REGULES LA PAZ · PLAZA GERTRUDIS BOCANEGRA · MARKET · LA BASILICA · LERIN · MUSEO DE ARTES POPULARES · TOURIST OFFICE · CALLE · LA COMPAÑIA CHURCH · PORTUGAL · JARDIN REVOLUTION · BAKERY · PLAZA VASCO DE QUIROGA · EL SANGRARIO · LAUNDROMAT · CASA DE ONCE PATIOS

This is also an area where a more recent tradition, the celebration of the Day of the Dead, is observed in spectacular fashion, particularly on the island of Janitzio. Entire Indian families pass the night of November 1 in the cemetery at the graves of loved ones, bringing offerings of food and flowers. Thousands of candles illuminate a night of music and prayers.

Accommodations
The most expensive hotels in downtown Pátzcuaro are cheap by American standards. On the Plaza Don Vasco the most attractive atmosphere and the best rooms are offered by the **Hotel Los Escudos** (tel. 2-01-38). The **Hotel Mesón del Gallo** (Doctor Cos #20, tel. 2-14-74) has elegant rooms and a swimming pool—a real bargain. For really cheap accommodations try the **Hotel Posada Imperial**, right past the Correo at Avenida Obregon #21 (tel. 2-03-08), sometimes noisy.

Food
The hole-in-the-wall **El Portal** (across from the Basilica) specializes in grilled meats—inexpensive quick service, three kinds of homemade salsa. **El Patio** on Plaza de Don Vasco offers cheap good meals in a more elegant environment. **Los Escudos**, also on the Plaza, has moderately-priced meals. **Las Redes** (The Nets) on the road to the Embarcadero has delicious budget meals and a pleasant atmosphere.

A Gentle Walk
Start your walk on the northern side of the Plaza Gertrudis Bocanegra de Laza de la Vega, named for a heroine of the war for independence who was shot in front of a tree on this square. Visit the public library, also named for her. After the library, turn left on Regules la Paz and walk uphill to the Basílica.

Making a left out of the Basílica, walk a block to the Museo de Artes Populares at the corner on the left. Across the street is the Iglesia de la Compañía. Continue two blocks on Calle Lerin to the Casa de Once Patios. Then retrace your steps half a block to El Sagrario.

Turn down Calle Portugal to the Plaza de Don Vasco de Quiroga, the spacious central plaza of the town.

Sightseeing Highlights
▲▲▲**Biblioteca Pública**—The former church of San Augustin, built in the 16th century, is now the public library. The huge mural by Juan O'Gorman depicts just about everything that has happened in this area in the last 400 years. Located on Plaza

Gertrudis Bocanegra. Open Mon.-Sat. 9:00 a.m.-7:00 p.m., Sun. 10:00 a.m.-1:00 p.m. and 3:00 p.m.-6:30 p.m.

▲▲**La Basílica**—Construction was begun in 1554, but this church was not consecrated until 1883. (Sounds like one of Steve's carpentry projects, Tina says.) The image of the Virgin Mary was made by the Indians in 1540 out of corn stalk paste, a technique of this area.

▲▲▲**Museo de Artes Populares** (Folk Art Museum)—The beautiful patio full of flowers complements the collection of fine weavings, woodwork and ceramics. See the miniature wax figures intricately clothed in Victorian styles, old retablos (paintings on wood attesting to miracles and healings), a feather "painting" of a monk and his dog, and a Day of the Dead altar. On Calle Lerin. Open Tue.-Sat. 9:00 a.m.-7:00 p.m., Sun. 9:00 a.m.-3:00 p.m., closed Mondays.

▲**Iglesia de la Compañía** (Company Church)—The first cathedral built in the state of Michoacán.

▲▲▲**Casa de Once Patios** (House of 11 Patios)—Formerly a convent, this building now houses small craft shops and *talleres* (workshops) where you can watch people weaving, doing lacquerware, etc. A good place to take photos. On Calle Lerin. Open daily 10:00 a.m.-2:00 p.m. and 4:00 p.m.-7:00 p.m.

▲▲**El Sagrario**—Pop into this old church to see its carved wooden pulpits, wooden parquet floor and golden stained glass window that looks like a sun. On Calle Lerin.

▲▲▲**Plaza de Don Vasco de Quiroga**—The main plaza is shaded by huge ash trees and surrounded by the portales of old colonial buildings now housing hotels, restaurants and the Tourist Information Office. A statue of Don Vasco marks the center of the plaza.

DAY 8
PATZCUARO-JANITZIO-MEXICO CITY

Today by intricate and clever scheduling you will visit the
Pátzcuaro market, take a boat ride on beautiful Lake Pátzcuaro
to the island of Janitzio and return to Mexico City in time for
dinner.

Suggested Schedule	
8:00	Breakfast in Pátzcuaro. Pack your bags for a quick afternoon departure.
9:00	Explore the market and enjoy the Plaza.
10:00	Take boat to Isla de Janitzio.
11:30	Early lunch on the island.
12:30	Boat trip back and return to hotel.
2:30	Depart for Morelia.
5:25	Catch Aeromexico Flight #143 to Mexico City.
6:30	Check into your Mexico City hotel and have dinner.

Getting to the Island of Janitzio
Take a cab or catch a bus marked "Lago" on Avenida las
Américas, to the *Embarcadero* (pier). Colorfully painted
canopied boats leave as they fill up, about one every twenty
minutes. The trip to the island takes half an hour. You'll have
about 1½ hours on the island.

Take the walk up to the big ugly statue of Morelos that domi-
nates the island and view the lake and other islands. Don't miss
the wild mural inside the statue. On your way up the winding
cobblestoned street you'll have had a chance to review all the
restaurants to select one for lunch. In picking a restaurant, a
good rule of thumb is to eat where the displayed chile rellenos
(stuffed chiles fried in batter) are the freshest and least greasy-
looking. The **Restaurant Janitzio**, the last restaurant on the
dock, to your left as you face the water, has very good local
pescado blanco (whitefish) and so-called *trucha* (trout). Steve
was actually served a bass. It's very Indian, with handmade tortillas and a view. For an even better view, try a restaurant up the
hill.

Bring some small bills, if you don't want to work off your
meal washing dishes! Restaurants often have trouble making
change, and a 5,000 peso note might as well be a hundred
dollar bill.

Getting Back to Mexico City

Take a bus to Morelia and then catch a cab to the airport, 20 km out of town. If you can't face a bus ride, and your pocket allows, hire a cab to take you straight to the Morelia airport from Pátzcuaro for about US $20. Hop aboard Aeromexico Flight #143.

Drivers can take the *Ruta Corta* (short route) to Mexico City via Morelia. In Morelia, follow the signs for Moravátio, then on to Atlacomulco, Toluca and the Mexico City airport to drop off your wheels.

Budget travelers can save the cost of air flight from Morelia to Mexico City by taking the first-class Tres Estrellas de Oro bus from Pátzcuaro at 2:10 p.m. arriving in Mexico City at 9:00 p.m.

In-Tour Extensions

If you have extra time, we recommend making a home base in Pátzcuaro and taking day trips to nearby villages.

Santa Clara del Cobre produces the beautiful copperwork you've seen in the Pátzcuaro market. You won't necessarily find better deals in the village, but you'll definitely see a wider selection. Start with the Museo del Cobre (Copper Museum) on the left side of the street just before the main square, open daily 9:00 a.m.-7:00 p.m. Walk around and visit the many shops. To see artisans at work, try the Casa Grande, about two blocks past the museum on the road to Pátzcuaro. Walk through the shop and straight to the back. Someone there will explain the process, in Spanish, if you ask. Santa Clara is about a 25-minute drive from Pátzcuaro, or you can catch a local bus.

Tzintzuntzan: This onomatopoetic Tarascan word means "Place of the Hummingbird". The village was once the capital of the province. Its central industry is the production of fanciful straw work. To get there, take the bus marked "Quiroga" from Pátzcuaro. On the right just before you get to town are the ruins of a pre-Hispanic city that was the center of an empire including the entire state of Michoacán. There's a great view of the lake from the ruins.

Train Trip

You may enjoy the leisurely overnight train ride to Mexico City, leaving Pátzcuaro at 9:25 p.m. and arriving at 8:00 a.m. Buy your tickets at the train station at 4:00 p.m. If you are traveling on a weekend, get them a couple of days ahead. (Note: don't take the train and then try to connect to the Mexico City-Oaxaca flight at 9:40 a.m. The schedule's too tight, and Mexican trains are often late.)

DAY 9
OAXACA

Today you'll take one giant step (by airplane) from central to southern Mexico. You'll immerse yourself in one of the most colorful marketplaces in all of Mexico and visit two fascinating museums displaying pre-Columbian treasure and artifacts. Round off your day watching a performance of regional folk dancing.

Suggested Schedule	
9:00	Check in at Mexico City Airport.
9:40	Flight to Oaxaca.
10:30	Take cab or rental car to hotel. If you're going to take a tour to the outlying villages tomorrow, make your arrangements now (see "Transportation," Day 10).
11:30	To Tianguis, the giant Saturday market. Prepare to be overwhelmed!
2:00	Back downtown for lunch and a snooze.
4:00	Walking Tour.
6:30	Dinner and bed, or see the folk dancers at Hotel Monte Albán.

Oaxaca Airport Orientation
When you arrive, before you do anything else, buy a taxi ticket at the counter with the sign *Boletos* (Tickets), near the luggage claim area. The only transportation into town is by colectivo. It costs around US $1.50 and will drop you at your hotel, but sometimes there isn't room for all the arrivals.

The airport Tourist Information Office will give you a package with a map of the city, information about the ruins in French, Spanish and butchered English, a list of hotels and a calendar in Spanish of the current cultural events.

Book a seat on Mexicana Flight #201 to Tuxtla Gutiérrez at 10:55 a.m. on Day 12 (next Tuesday).

If you want to rent a car there are several rental agencies at the airport and one downtown.

Oaxaca
Twenty years ago, when we first saw the purple blossoms of the jacaranda trees against the deep blue of the sky, we fell in love with Oaxaca and its valley. Nature's dramatic setting for the city of Oaxaca is a broad fertile plain surrounded on all sides by mountains. Equally dramatic and colorful are the Indians of the

more than seventy tribes in the state, many of whom continue to dress in their distinctive *traje* (traditional Indian dress). This beautiful clothing is a feast for the eyes in the marketplace, on the backs of ordinary people rather than in a museum. Oaxaca's exciting market is one of the best places in Mexico to shop for clothing, rugs and blankets, and such unusual items as carved gourd rattles and bamboo drums, all made by Zapotec and Mixtec Indians.

The hub of life is the zócalo. Oaxaca's large and stately public garden, with its white latticework bandstand and surrounding sidewalk cafes, is a center of bustling activity all day and late into the night. Oaxaca is also politically active, and the last few times we've been there thousands of teachers paraded around the zócalo, bearing banners and chanting *"¡País petrolero, pueblo sin dinero!"* (A country with oil, the people without money!).

Oaxaca (from an Aztec word meaning "place of the gourds") was founded in 1532. Altitude: 5,000 ft. Population: 240,000.

Accommodations

The best place to stay in town is the **El Presidente** (Calle 5 de Mayo #300, tel. 6-06-11). Located in the ex-Convent of Santa Catalina, this is one of the most beautiful hotels in Mexico, slightly above our price range for deluxe hotels. Even if you're not staying there, it's worth visiting for buffet breakfast or a drink. Also very nice are the **Marqués del Valle** on the zócalo (tel. 6-31-98) and the **Monte Albán** (#1 Calle de León, tel. 6-37-77).

A good moderately priced hotel is the **Plaza** (Trujano #112, tel. 6-40-20). We also like the **Hotel Antiquera** (Av. Hidalgo #807, tel. 6-40-20). Not as central, the **Meson del Angel** (Mina #518, tel. 6-66-66) boasts a large swimming pool.

Our favorite budget hotel is the **Del Valle** (205 Díaz Ordaz. Be careful not to confuse it with another hotel of the same name on Aldama). Get a third floor room; there's a nice terrace.

Food

Oaxaca isn't one of our favorite eating towns, but it offers a distinctive regional cuisine. This is the land of black beans and huge corn tortillas called *blanditas* ("little softies," though they're neither little nor particularly soft). Oaxaca is famous for its many varieties of *mole* sauce—some are *picante* (hot), all are flavorful. The *fondas* (market restaurants) in the downtown market are a good place for the adventurous to try out some regional specialties. Be sure to ask the price first. There are no menus and fondas sometimes overcharge tourists.

Our best meal in Oaxaca was at the **Restaurant Ajos y**

Cebollas (Garlic and Onions), Calle de la Alameda #605 across from Juárez Park. They serve excellent meats, pastas and seafood. There is a bar and live music at night. Try the filete Tampiqueña if you are a steak eater. The **Restaurant Catedral**, just two blocks from the zócalo on Morelos at Garcia Vigil, is clean and pleasant with decent food and fast service.

Vegetarians will want to try **El Arco de Emmanuel** on Calzada Chapultapec #1023. They also have a health food store.

Try the **D'Artagnan** (1011 Hidalgo) for an international menu, moderately expensive.

One of our favorite Oaxacan restaurants is the **Coronita** in the Hotel del Valle (Diáz Ordaz #208, ½ block off Hidalgo), featuring well-prepared regional cuisine at quite moderate prices; the afternoon comida corrida is excellent. You'll also find good moderately priced traditional Oaxacan food in a slightly funky but pretty colonial patio at **Restaurant Típico de Oaxaca** (Calle Antonia Labastida #118, near Hotel Presidente).

For a quick tasty lunch in a Mexican version of a fast food restaurant, go to **El Mesón** on Hidalgo just off the zócalo. They serve Oaxacan dishes, pozole and tacos.

Quench your thirst with a fresh juice or *liquado* (smoothie) at **Jugos La Tropical** on the corner of Garcia and Mina near the Mercado de Artesanías. Very clean. Desserts, too.

Several popular tourist restaurants in the portales around the zócalo tend to be expensive with slow service, but they're good for people-watching. You can order a beer or soda, enjoy the atmosphere and save your eating for better places.

Oaxaca Walking Tour
Leaving the Cathedral, walk up Macedonio Alcalá, which is pleasantly blocked off from traffic, to the astounding Templo de Santo Domingo de Guzman. Visit the Regional Museum next door. Continue half a block up Macedonio Alcalá and make a left, walking through the Plazuela del Carmen del Alto. Make a right at the next corner and go half a block up the street to the Benito Juárez Museum on the left. Turn back down Vigil to Avenida Morelos, then make a right and walk two blocks to the Museo de Arte Prehispánico de México Rufino Tamayo. Continue in the same direction on Morelos, and just after Unión turn left into the complex of La Iglesia de la Soledad.

Sightseeing Highlights
▲**La Catedral**—Located next to the zócalo, this massive cathedral was begun in 1533 but was damaged several times by earthquakes and rebuilt in a variety of styles. On the main altar is a bronze statue of the Virgin by the Italian sculptor Tadolini.

▲▲▲Museo Regional de Oaxaca—This fascinating museum, housed in a beautiful former convent adjoining Santo Domingo church, has sections devoted to fine old examples of regional dress, ancient ceramics and gorgeous jewelry from Monte Albán's Tomb #7 (false fingernails made of gold). Skulls dating to the third epoch give evidence that this sophisticated culture experimented with brain surgery.

▲▲▲Templo de Santo Domingo (Santo Domingo Church)— Begun in 1551 by Dominican friars with only 2 ½ pesos in their treasury, it was finally finished in 1666. The baroque gilded decoration of the interior defies description. The arched ceiling of the entranceway is covered by what appears to be an elegant depiction of the Tree of Life. It is, in fact, the family tree of Don Felix de Guzman, father of the Dominicans' founder. Designated a National Monument in 1976, this church is one of the most important architectural works in the Americas. Even if churches bore you, don't miss it.

▲▲Museo Benito Juárez—Juárez, often called the Abraham Lincoln of Mexico, was a Zapotec Indian who became president of Mexico when the French were driven out in the 1860s. He instituted many liberal reforms, as well as ordering the execution of the Emperor Maximillian by firing squad. Juárez lived in this simple house for twelve years when he first moved to Oaxaca from his native village. Open Tue.-Sun. 10:00 a.m.-2:30 p.m. and 3:30-7:00 p.m.

▲▲▲Museo de Arte Prehispanico de Mexico Rufino Tamayo—The famous Oaxacan painter Rufino Tamayo collected these pre-Columbian artifacts over a twenty-year period and donated them to the people of Oaxaca—an exquisite museum. Open 10:00 a.m.-2:00 p.m. and 4:00 p.m.-7:00 p.m., closed Tuesdays.

▲▲La Iglesia de la Soledad (Church of Solitude)—Legend has it that this old church was founded on the spot where a mule carrying a big load lay down and refused to move. The muleteer opened the cargo and discovered an image of the Virgin. The mule was dead. The Virgin is displayed in the church. Check out the 2-kilo gold crown decorated with 600 diamonds!

Oaxaca Saturday Market (Tianguis)

Until recently the tianguis was held in the downtown streets. Though it lost a little flavor since moving to modern quarters on the edge of town, it's much easier to find your way around and still rates as one of the most interesting and largest Indian markets in all of Latin America. You'll find arts and crafts from throughout the region on sale. If you're interested in buying a rug or blanket, wait until you visit Teotitlán del Valle where they are made.

DAY 10
TLACOLULA & RUINS

Today's action-packed schedule will take you to an Indian
market at an outlying village, several important and striking
Zapotec ruins, a town famous for its woven rugs and blankets.
Finish up with a visit to one of the largest and oldest trees in the
Americas.

Suggested Schedule	
9:00	Take transportation of choice to Sunday market in Tlacolula.
11:00	Mitla. See the ruins and shop. Visit the museum.
1:30	Lunch at Museo Frissell in the village.
2:30	Visit the ruins of Yagul.
3:30	Visit the shops and homes of rug makers in Teotitlán del Valle.
5:00	See the ruins of Dainzú and the Tule Tree on your way back to Oaxaca.
6:00	Dinner and join the Sunday evening promenade on the zócalo.

Transportation
You can do the trip by bus, but we don't recommend it because
you'll be visiting so many places. Instead, hire a cab for the day
(US $25-30) or take a guided tour from a travel agency in Hotel
Presidente, Hotel Marqués del Valle or Hotel Señorial. Check a
day ahead, as you may need reservations.
  Drivers, follow the signs on Highway 190.

Sightseeing Highlights
  ▲▲▲**Mitla**—This Zapotec archaeological site was occupied
as early as 100 A.D. Later, when Monte Albán was abandoned,
Mitla became the valley's most important center. The ruins
feature elaborate geometric ornamentation. There are two main
groups: the Church Group and the Column Group. The name
"Mitla" comes from a Náhuatl word meaning "Place of the
Dead." Open daily 8:00 a.m.-6:00 p.m.
  ▲▲▲**Museo Frissell**—Located downtown near the small
plaza, this museum has a very good collection of local artifacts.
Open daily 9:00 a.m.-6:00 p.m. The museum restaurant serves
lunch at 1:30 p.m.
  Much of the clothing sold in Oaxaca city comes from Mitla.
You can get a slightly better price here, but you have to work at

it. There's a market near the ruins, and lots of shops in the village.

▲▲Yagul—1,400-year-old ruins on a hillside command a beautiful view of the valley. There are three tombs and a big stone frog representing the rain god. Open daily 9:00 a.m.-6:00 p.m.

▲▲▲Teotitlán del Valle—This Zapotec Indian village is world famous for its weavings. Influenced by innovative buyers' requests, craftspeople have been weaving reproductions of works by such painters as Escher and Picasso as well as continuing to produce their own beautiful designs. If you want 100% wool, examine your choice in the sunlight and look for the telltale shine of acrylic. Many weavers use a blend.

▲Dainzú—This large ruin is only partially reconstructed. Interesting rock carvings.

▲▲The Tule Tree—The circumference of this magnificent 2,000-year-old tree is greater than its 125-foot height. It deserves at least a salute, if not some outright tree worship.

DAY 11

OAXACA-MONTE ALBAN

After a late breakfast and an easy morning poking around markets, you'll spend the afternoon in the Zapotec ruin of Monte Albán, overlooking the valley of Oaxaca. Let your children, or the child inside you, play in the tunnels and hidden passageways.

Suggested Schedule	
9:00	After a leisurely breakfast (such as the buffet at Hotel Presidente) spend the morning shopping in the Benito Juárez Market downtown and at the nearby Mercado de Artesanías.
12:00	Lunch downtown. If you aren't hungry, pick up some snacks to take along as there are only sodas at the ruins.
12:30	Leave for Monte Albán. Allow at least 3 hours to see these ruins.
6:00	Dinner downtown. If you have any energy left, check out Oaxaca's nightlife.

Sightseeing Highlights

▲▲▲**Mercado Benito Juárez**—Located near the zócalo. This old market is an excellent place to buy local arts and crafts and handwoven clothing. You will have to bargain hard, but a fair deal for all concerned can be had. If an occasional vendor is surly or gets angry when you offer to bargain, just move on. Oaxaca is one of the few places in Mexico where you sometimes encounter unfriendly people, especially in the markets. Don't take it personally; Mexicans from other parts of the country tell us they get the same treatment. Fortunately, most Oaxacans are friendly.

▲▲**Mercado de Artesanías** (Arts and Crafts Market)—This market has a large selection of local artesanía but it tends to be more expensive than other markets. Still worth a look.

Transportation

Monte Albán is a half-hour drive from Oaxaca, six miles—straight up. Rental car people, follow your map and be very careful on the curves. *Colectivos* (mini-buses) leave for the ruins from the Hotel Mesón del Angel (Mina #518) at 9:30 a.m., 10:30 a.m., 11:30 a.m., 12:30 p.m. and 3:30 p.m. They sell round trip tickets and stay only 1½ hours, so if you want to stay longer you'll have to buy two tickets and return on a later bus. Tickets are about US $1. Other alternatives are to hire a cab or go on a guided tour, offered by several travel agencies in town. Check at the Hotel Presidente, Hotel Marqués del Vale or Hotel Señorial for information.

Monte Albán

On a mountaintop overlooking the entire Oaxaca Valley, Monte Albán is one of Mexico's most impressive ruins. The site was occupied for over 1,200 years, from 500 B.C. to 750 A.D. when most of the inhabitants apparently abandoned them. The Zapotecs who built these temples and ceremonial center are the ancestors of the valley's present-day Indian population, many of whom still speak the ancient Zapotec language. Be sure to see Tomb 104 with its beautifully preserved wall paintings. If it's closed when you get to it, try again later.

The ruins and adjoining museum are open daily from 8:00 a.m. to 5:00 p.m. Guide service is available at the museum in English, French or Spanish for about US $3 for one person and US $1 for each additional person. Buy a guidebook in English at the museum shop if you don't hire a guide. The museum also has a tourist information booth.

Hint: Wear casual clothes and walking shoes, and bring a flashlight if you like poking around in tunnels and underground passages.

Walk through the Ruins

After buying your ticket at the museum, walk up the road to the main entrance. On your left as you enter the **Great Plaza** is the

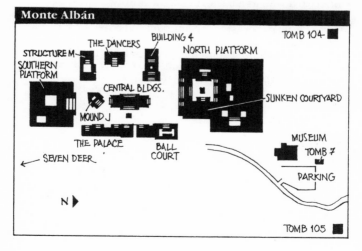

Ball Court. This court lacks the stone hoops or rings of the later Toltec game courts. The steps on either side of the court probably served to hold the stucco facing in place. Continuing along the eastern side of the plaza you will find platforms that served as housing and two temples. The first of these pyramids has an interior stairway to the top as well as an underground tunnel linking it to the center buildings.

The three linked **Central Buildings** contain an altar where the famous jade bat mask was found. The fourth central building, called **Mound J**, is arrow-shaped and decorated with sculptural glyphs. At the southern end of the plaza, appropriately enough, you'll find the **Southern Platform**, one for true climbers. The hike to the top provides a remarkable view of the Plaza and surrounding countryside, including the complex of buildings to the southeast called **Seven Deer**, named for the glyph on its lintel. Continue clockwise to the buildings on the western side of the plaza. The first, **Structure M**, has a central stairway topped by four pillars. The next building is **Los Danzantes**, the famed building of the Dancers, named for the series of slabs carved with human figures in various attitudes. Many of these figures have strongly negroid features and are cited by some to support the theory of an ancient seeding of Mexico by the Phoenicians of Africa. On the northwest end of the plaza is **Building 4**, with an altar in the central patio and a tunnel excavated to reveal an earlier building. The stairway of the **Northern Platform** has a sanctuary on either side; the eastern one has a number of reliefs and **Stele 9**, sculpted on four sides. At the top of the stairway are two rows of columns and the **Sunken Courtyard** with its altar. A path to the northwest leads you to **Tomb 104**; all four of its interior walls are covered with murals. On your walk back east to the museum and parking lot you will come to **Tomb 7**, where the treasures exhibited in the Oaxaca Museum were found. East of the road that leads to Monte Albán is **Tomb 105**, also famous for its interior murals. The trick to visiting these tombs is finding out when they are *really* open.

In-Tour Extensions:

The Oaxaca Valley
If you love Oaxaca like we love Oaxaca, you won't want to tear yourself away after a mere two days. There's enough to keep you here for at least a week. If you stay longer, however, be sure to plan your extension around the available flights to Tuxtla Gutiérrez. There are only three flights weekly—on Tuesday, Thursday and Saturday, all on Mexicana airlines.

Check the market list at the back of this book. You can enjoy an Indian market any day of the week in or near Oaxaca City; some days have two or three to choose from.

San Bartolo Coyotepec is worth a visit any day of the week. Visit the *alfarería* (pottery studio) of the famous Doña Rosa, who died in 1981. Her son Valente Nieto Real continues making pottery and does pottery demonstrations on request. The courtyard has shelves of pottery for sale and a gallery of framed photographs and newspaper articles about Doña Rosa on the wall. (On a Friday, you could combine a trip to San Bartolo Coyotepec with a trip to the market at **Ocotlán de Morelos**.)

Oaxaca's Pacific Coast-Puerto Escondido

Puerto Escondido is just a hop, skip and jump by air from the valley of Oaxaca. Once a tiny fishing village, it is now a popular tourist spot, with sports fishing and tours available by boat and horseback. This is a handy place to fit in a few extra days on the beach. There are two flights daily from Oaxaca City on Oaxaca-Aerovias Oaxaqueños airlines. Their office is near the zócalo in Oaxaca at Armente y Lopez #209.

Accommodations: One of the more elegant hotels in Puerto Escondido is the **Hotel Santa Fé**, Calle del Morro (tel. 2-01-70), overlooking the ocean at the southeastern tip of the bay. It has a swimming pool, craft and clothing shop and a nice restaurant. The best deal in town is the **Hotel Rincon del Pacifico**, centrally located on the main street at Avenida Perez Gasca #900 (tel. 2-00-56). Big airy rooms surround a courtyard of palm trees, and its restaurant is one of the best in town. Steve's friend señor Cortez, the local pharmacist, recommends the *huachinango al horno* (baked red snapper). On the same street, up the hill, are the moderately priced **Hotel Loren** and the **Hotel Nayer**. The **Hotel Villa Marinero**, on the beach (tel. 2-01-80) has cabañas that sleep up to four, with kitchens. If you're a frustrated cook, tired of too much restaurant eating, this is a good place to stay home for breakfast.

Restaurants: We recommend the **Restaurant Hipocampo**. Steve also likes the **Il Cappuccino** for breakfast—great fruit salads.

What to do: Hit the beach. You needn't bring along a mid-morning snack: just as hunger starts to strike, a beach vendor is likely to pop up selling bags of peanuts, *gelatinas* (Jello cups), sweet tamales or corn-on-the-cob. In fact, you can spend your entire day looking at jewelry, hammocks and even clothing. Of course, this can get somewhat annoying, if you're into gazing and daydreaming or reading a good novel instead of shopping.

There are more secluded beaches in the area. You can walk to Playa Zicatela, the next beach south, and get away from some of the madness. There are also tours to various beaches and lagunas; check with Turismo Manacar, at Av. Perez Gasga #302, or FCQ's Travel Service at Av. Perez Gasga and Andador Libertad.

A word to the wise: Women should not walk alone on the beach here at night. There is also petty thievery, even during the day.

DAY 12
TRAVEL TO SAN CRISTOBAL

Today will be a "hard travelin'" day. Most of your time and energy will be spent getting from Oaxaca via Tuxtla Gutiérrez to San Cristóbal de las Casas, where you'll enter the world of the Highland Mayas.

Suggested Schedule	
8:30	Breakfast in Oaxaca.
10:00	Check in at airport and catch Mexicana Flight #201 to Tuxtla Gutiérrez at 10:55.
Noon	Take cab to bus station in Tuxtla, check bags and have lunch nearby or on main square. Or, if you are renting a car to go to San Cristóbal, rent it at the Tuxtla airport.
2:00	Bus to San Cristóbal de las Casas.
4:00	Arrive in San Cristóbal and check into hotel. Rest!
6:00	Dinner.

Transportation: Tuxtla Gutiérrez to San Cristóbal
Catch a colectivo into Tuxtla Gutiérrez from the airport for about US $2. Taxis cost about US $5 for a maximum of two people.

Go to the Cristóbal Colón bus station at Av. 2da Norte and Calle Poniente. Check your luggage and buy tickets for the 2:00 p.m. bus to San Cristóbal. Have lunch at one of the restaurants within easy walking distance on the main drag, Av. 14 de Septiembre.

If you rent a car at the Tuxtla Gutiérrez airport, you'll also have to drive *back* from San Cristóbal, drop your car at the airport again, and fly to Villahermosa—where you'll rent another car to go to Palenque. If that's your preference, make a reservation on Aeromexico Flight #516 to Villahermosa, leaving at 2:30 p.m. on Day 14 (two days from today).

For people in cars: About 20 minutes out of Tuxtla on the road to San Cristóbal is a sign for the "Chorreadero." The waterfall from a cave into a series of pools is well worth a look and even a refreshing swim, if you're a polar bear.

San Cristóbal de las Casas
Altitude 6,800 feet, population 40,000. This highland Mayan town is only 87 miles from the Guatemalan frontier, and its

cultural connections with the neighboring country are evident
to anyone who has traveled farther south. You will find Indians
tenaciously maintaining their traditions. The state of Chiapas is
one of the few remaining areas in Mexico where Indian *men*
continue to dress in traditional village *traje*. They look impressive. It's hard to believe that men dressed in bright pink
ponchos, pants like white pedal-pushers and straw hats fes-
tooned with ribbon streamers could maintain their dignity, but
they certainly do. The highland Mayan Indians sell traditional
clothing, woolen ponchos and nice leatherwork. Some of Mexico's finest textile work is done in the San Cristóbal area. You
will also find Guatemalan weavings.

The beautiful mountainous countryside is highly cultivated.
Little *milpas* (corn fields) crisscross the outrageously steep
slopes, often causing Steve to exclaim, "Aren't you glad you
don't have to water *that*!" To the Indians, a piece of earth,
however small and inaccessible, is precious and to be cultivated
with care. Many of them derive their only livelihood selling
small crops of corn or vegetables from these plots.

The town of San Cristóbal was founded in 1528. Each of its
several *barrios* (neighborhoods) spoke a different language and
had its own church. Each barrio tended to have its own specialty, such as raising pigs, weaving, fireworks-making or masonry.
What is now the market area formerly specialized in candy and
sweets. There were the toymakers of Guadalupe, the potters of
San Ramón, the woodcutters, charcoal-makers and launderers
of Santa Lupe. Some deep-rooted traditions persist, but today
the mule drivers of San Diego deliver merchandise to nearby
villages by pickup truck.

Accommodations

The most expensive hotel in town is not as nice as the **Hotel
Español** (1ro de Marzo #16, tel. 8-00-45) which has big rooms
with fireplaces, a feature you may want to take advantage of in
this town. The **Santa Clara**, on the corner of the plaza (Av. Insurgentes #1, tel. 8-11-40) is the 16th century former home of
Diego de Mazariezgo. The hotel has a lot of charm, with colorful red macaws in the patio. The warmest rooms are on the
third floor.

Almost next door, the **Hotel de Ciudad Real** (Plaza 31 de
Mayo #10, tel. 8-01-87) is just as nice and a better deal. It has a
very pretty roofed courtyard restaurant with flowers, ferns and
a small parrot. Also in the moderate price range are **Hotel
Palacio de Moctezuma** (Av. Juárez #16, tel. 8-03-52) and the
Hotel Fray Bartolome de las Casas (Niños Héroes #2, tel.
8-09-32).

The best budget accommodations are found at the **Hotel San Martín**, ½ block east of the jardín (Calle Real de Guadalupe #16, tel. 8-05-33).

Food

San Cristóbal is not a great "eating town," but it has the distinction of being one of the least expensive places to eat in all of Mexico. For an elegant dining room overlooking the zócalo, try the restaurant **La Plaza**, whose entrance is at Hidalgo #1. The comida corrida is expensive for San Cristóbal, but the entrees are quite reasonable and very good.

Another favorite of ours is the restaurant of the **Hotel Palacio de Moctezoma** (Av. Juárez #7)—very pretty courtyard, good food, moderate prices, what more could you ask for? The **Restaurant El Tuluc** on Madero a block up from the zócalo has a good comida corrida between 1:00 and 5:00 p.m.

Normitás on Juárez at Dr. Flores has a rustic atmosphere, with tables made from slabs of log. It doesn't open until 1:00 p.m. and is closed on Sundays. For a quick breakfast or lunch, try **Los Arcos** just off the zócalo on Madero. The hip coffee house in town is **La Galería**, Hidalgo #3, with a gallery/boutique downstairs, coffee upstairs.

Helpful Hints

The Tourist Office on the northwest corner of the plaza has lots of photo displays, maps and information on nearby villages. They also have the phonograph that plays piped-in music on the plaza. Check out their records and see if there's a favorite you'd like them to play.

Shopping: Look for leatherwork, handsome and simple woolen ponchos, primitive dolls and Guatemalan crafts. We like to buy dolls and the simpler woolen weavings from the women on the street and in the plaza in front of Santo Domingo church. On the main square, you will find yourself surrounded by Indian ladies waving woven bracelets and anklets in your face. We're always sorry we can't buy something from everybody.

DAY 13

SAN CRISTOBAL DE LAS CASAS

Today you'll explore San Cristóbal, admire (and perhaps buy) the textiles of an Indian weaving cooperative and visit the home of the famous archaeologists Frans Blom and Gertrude Duby.

Suggested Schedule	
9:00	Breakfast.
10:00	Walking Tour.
2:00	Lunch and free time for shopping.
4:00	Cab to Casa Na-Bolom and take tour.
5:30	Get bus tickets to Palenque for tomorrow morning at 8:30 a.m. If you are planning a side trip to Bonampak and Yaxchilán (see "In-tour Extension," Day 15), phone ahead for reservations.
6:00	Dinner.

Walking Tour
Starting at the Cathedral, notable for its carved wooden ceilings and the birds living in it, take Calle Utrilla toward the market, visiting shops on the way. Explore the market and pick up some snacks for tomorrow's trip. Now retrace your steps on Utrilla and turn right on Comitán, into the complex of the Templo y Convento de Santo Domingo. Next door to the church is the weavers' cooperative of Santa Jolobil. Return to the plaza and walk three blocks past it, making a right on Calle Hermanos Domínguez. Look inside the Templo de Carmen. Across the little plaza is an oddly shaped modern building, the concert hall of the School of Bellas Artes. If classes are in session, take a look around. On Hermanos Domínguez make a left. It's two blocks to the staircase climbing to the Templo de San Cristóbal and El Mirador. Enjoy the 360-degree view and bring your heart rate back down to normal. Returning to the plaza, you might want to explore the shops on Calle Real de Guadalupe.

Bus Tickets
The bus station is on Ignacio Allende at the Periférico (bypass around town). The first class bus line is the Tuxtla. The trip to Palenque takes about 6 hours and costs less than US $3.

Sightseeing Highlights
▲**Cathedral**—Check out the ornate baroque altarpiece.

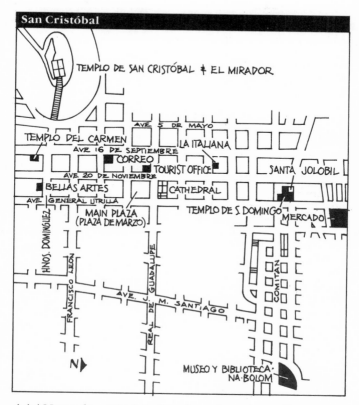

▲▲▲Mercado—Watch Indians from the various villages congregate to sell their wares, do their shopping and exchange news. If you need an excuse to stand around and stare, buy an *elote* (corn on a stick, with or without chile and lime) or a bag of peanuts to munch on.

▲▲▲Templo de Santo Domingo—The walls and pulpit of this 16th century church are encrusted with gold. There is a smell of copal incense, a tree sap used by the Indians as an offering since ancient times. The floral decorations are elaborate and lovely. If you're lucky, you may happen upon an Indian *curandero* (healer) doing a *limpia* (cleansing) on a client. We watched a curandero here use eggs for the cleansing, chanting prayers with many candles burning on the floor around them.

▲▲▲Santa Jolobil—Housed in the former convent of the church, this weaving cooperative is run by Tzotzil and Tzeltal Mayan traditional artists. The members are dedicated to reviving the former quality of the textile arts and use very old designs. It is also a study center for the technique of brocade. Though the works on display are high-priced by Mexican standards, the quality is unsurpassed. An elaborate *huipil* (blouse) takes many months to make, and the weavers only earn a minimum wage.

▲**Templo del Carmen**—The oldest church in San Cristóbal.

▲**Casa de la Cultura** and **Concert Hall**—This art school offers classes in classical guitar, dance, etc. Check the posters on the concert hall to see if there is a concert happening while you're in town.

▲▲**Templo de San Cristóbal** and **El Mirador**—You're there for the view and the exercise.

▲▲▲**Na-Bolom**—Tour the home of archaeologists and anthropologists Frans Blom and Gertrude Duby, who have worked since the 1950s with the Lacandón Indians, the last remaining tribes of jungle Indians in Mexico. Frans Blom died in 1963, but his wife has continued with their work. Besides documenting customs and traditions, she has fought to preserve the threatened rain forest domain of the Lacandóns. The tour includes the small museum and library of over 13,000 volumes on Meso-america, the garden, the chapel and the Lacandón sala. Open for tours Tue.-Sun., 4:00 p.m.-5:30 p.m. The library is open Tue.-Sat. 9:00 a.m.-1:30 p.m., Mon. 2:30 p.m.-6:00 p.m. Closed Sunday. Donations are appreciated.

In-Tour Extensions:

Rent a horse and ride to one of the nearby villages. Horse rentals are available through the Casa de Huespedes Margarita at Calle Real de Guadalupe #34 or through the Posada Diego de Mazariegos at 5 de Febrero #1. Take a 4 to 6 hour trip with a guide to either the Grutas (caves) or to San Juan Chamula. It's best to make arrangements a day in advance.

The Posada Diego de Mazriegos travel agency also offers tours by VW bus to San Juan Chamula, Zinacantán and the Grutas or to the Lagos de Montebello (Lakes of the Pretty Mountain). These 8-hour tours are for a minimum of 4 persons.

Combis leave from the market area in San Cristóbal all the time for nearby villages; just find the mini-bus marked with the name of the town you want to explore and hop aboard for a real Indian adventure.

A word to the wise: The Indians of San Juan de Chamula do not want to be photographed. Like many Indians, they believe that the camera captures their soul. It is illegal to take photographs, *strictly enforced*!

DAY 14
TRAVEL TO PALENQUE

After traveling from highland San Cristóbal to Palenque in the jungle lowlands of Chiapas, you'll relax in a pool and adjust to the sudden descent and tropical climate. You may have the good fortune to glimpse Lacandón Indians, the last tribal inhabitants of the Mexican rain forest, come to town to shop and trade.

Suggested Schedule	
8:30	Bus departs for the town of Palenque. The ruins of Palenque are 5 miles out of town. (Drivers—see Alternate Plan.)
2:30	Arrive in Palenque, voracious! Check into hotel and get some lunch (or vice versa).
4:00	Cool off in the hotel swimming pool.
5:00	Make arrangements for afternoon tour tomorrow to Agua Azul. Look around town.
6:30	Dinner.
	Alternate Plan—Drivers
8:00	Drive to Tenejapa (about 45 minutes from San Cristóbal) for market day. The road is rough but passable.
9:00	Visit the market, church, Museo Regional and Sociedad Cooperativa de Artesanías, if they are open (erratic hours).
10:30	Return to San Cristóbal.
11:30	Drive to Tuxtla Guttiérrez.
1:30	Lunch at Airport.
2:30	Take Aeromexico Flight #516 to Villahermosa.
3:30	Rent car at Villahermosa airport and drive to Palenque.
5:30	Arrive in Palenque and check into hotel.
6:30	Dinner.

Accommodations
When we first went to Palenque the town was a dirt street village with virtually no accommodations. That has certainly changed. Now you can find a full range of hotels from the budget **Hotel Palenque** right off the plaza (Av. 5 de Mayo #14)

to beautiful, moderately expensive bungalows at **Hotel Chan Kah** on the road to the ruins (Km. 3). It boasts a beautiful garden with pet monkeys. We highly recommend the **Hotel Cañada** (Calle Merle Green), in town but located in a jungle-like wooded area—nice bungalows quite reasonably priced, but unfortunately often full. **Las Ruinas** at Km. 6 on the road to the ruins is moderately priced, with a good swimming pool which you'll really appreciate in this hot humid climate. The lowest-priced budget hotel we've found is the **Hotel La Croix** (Av. Hidalgo #18)—the beds aren't great, but there are nice murals on the walls.

Food

There are several good restaurants in and around the town of Palenque. You'll begin to notice the Yucatán Maya influence in the cooking. A very moderately priced restaurant right off the zócalo is the **Restaurant Maya**—clean with a bar and Mayan specialties. Two other in-town restaurants we like are **La Cañada** (at the aforementioned Hotel Cañada) and the nearby **Restaurant La Selva**. Both have moderate prices, bars and jungle atmosphere. On the road to the ruins the attractive **Restaurant El Paraíso** (Paradise) has moderately priced meals, a bar and marimba players. Take a cab to this one if you're not driving a car, or catch one of the VW bus collectivos.

DAY 15
PALENQUE

Palenque is among the loveliest of all Mayan ruins, and today is your chance to enjoy it. In the afternoon you'll visit the magnificent waterfalls of Agua Azul.

Suggested Schedule	
8:00	Be at the ruins when they open. Explore the Temple of the Sun complex and the Palace.
9:45	Take the jungle path to the Lion Temple.
10:00	Be at the top of the Temple of the Inscriptions when they open the tomb.
10:30	Visit Northern Group, Ball Park and Museum.
12:00	Lunch.
1:00	Tour or taxi to the waterfalls of Misol-Ha and Agua Azul.
7:00	Dinner.

Palenque Ruins

The Mayan civilization encompassed the entire Yucatán peninsula of Mexico, parts of the state of Chiapas, all of Guatamala, Belize and the northwestern sections of Honduras and El Salvador. There is evidence of nomadic peoples in the area as early as 10,000 B.C., and Mayan civilization reached its height between A.D. 300 and 900, the Classic Period. Around A.D. 900 the great ceremonial centers mysteriously fell into disuse.

The Mayas were the only people in the Americas to develop writing, though many of their inscriptions remain undeciphered. Study has revealed that most of the carved stone records are calendars marking time by days, months, *tuns* (years), *katuns* (20-year periods) and *baktuns* (twenty 20-year cycles). Time and the gods were entwined concepts: each day was a god, and the rich Mayan ceremonial life centered around their calendar and the cycles of the planets. The astrologer-priests, meticulous observers of the movement of the planets, chose auspicious times to clear the forests and plant and harvest crops. The Mayan gods were the forces of nature personified—the sun, the rain, the earth and other planets.

Against the lush green jungle, the elegant tracery of the roof-combs of Palenque's Temple of the Sun and the Temple of the Inscriptions lend an almost Oriental air to the site. If you arrive early in the morning you will have the great pleasure of experiencing the mood of the ruins and the jungle undisturbed by the noise of tourism.

There are two ways to approach a ruin. (1) The academician, armed with guidebooks, maps, field glasses and flashlight, comes determined to appraise, compare, collect data—in short, to research it. (2) The "feeler" drifts through on the atmosphere of the place and absorbs ancient vibes. We've found that it's possible to harmoniously blend both types of experience by becoming knowledgable about the site, then climbing to the top of a temple to enjoy the view and settle into quiet contemplation. In that way both the scientist and the poet in each of us are satisfied.

Getting to the Ruins

Collective taxis to the ruins leave town every 15 minutes from the office of Colectivos Chambalu, off Benito Juárez on Ignacio Allende street. Flag one down on the street, or on the highway if you're staying near the ruins. ADO bus lines has a first class bus to the ruins daily at 10:00 a.m. Cabs charge about US $2.

Seeing the Ruins

If you're lucky, there will be Lacandón Indians at the entrance dressed in their simple white robes, selling large bows and arrows trimmed with parrot feathers. Even if you can't fit a set in your suitcase, be sure to examine their wares and give yourself the opportunity to talk with these handsome open-faced men (if only in sign language).

Walk straight in past the Temple of the Inscriptions on your right and the Palace with its tower on your left (we'll get back to these later) and cross the **Aqueduct**. On the right is the **Temple of the Sun**, which you'll climb to see the magnificent carved panel, representing the sun being worshipped by two priests, on the back wall of the shrine.

The **Temple of the Foliated Cross** faces the Temple of the Sun. The panel for which this temple was named shows a cross decorated with corn leaves and human heads. The sun god and a quetzal bird with the mask of the rain god surmount the cross. The decorative crosses at Palenque are thought to be stylized versions of the corn plant, much venerated by the early Mayas and still addressed as "Your Grace" by Indians today. Or they may represent the ceiba tree, the sacred tree believed to stand at the four corners of the world and at the center of the universe.

Your third climb of the day (Hey, you're just getting started!) will be to the top of the **Temple of the Cross**. Finish up this group with **Temple 14** on your right as you head back to the Palace.

The **Palace** complex bears some exploring. Use your flashlight in the cellars on the southern side. The tower has an interior

Palenque

TO PALENQUE →

N

NORTHERN GROUP

TEMPLE OF THE COUNT

MUSEUM

BALL COURT

PALACE

POOL AND PATH

ENTRANCE

TEMPLE OF THE INSCRIPTIONS

AQUADUCT

TEMPLE 14

TEMPLE OF THE CROSS

STAIRCASE

TEMPLE OF THE LION

TEMPLE OF THE SUN

TEMPLE OF THE FOLIATED CROSS

staircase that starts on the second floor, which you reach from the north side.

There is a small staircase in the hillside behind the Temple of the Inscriptions. Follow it and the path to the **Temple of the Lion**. When you return, enter the top of the **Temple of the Inscriptions** from the hillside behind it, avoiding the steepest climb in the ruins. The panel to which this temple owes its name is now preserved in the National Museum of Anthropology in Mexico City. The panels on either side of the sanctuary door are well preserved. One depicts an old priest, draped in a tiger skin, smoking a cigar. The staircase and the funerary crypt were discovered in 1952. The body inside was interred under a gigantic carved slab. Also found here was a magnificent jade mask, since stolen from the National Museum of Anthropology.

Next, visit the **Ball Court**, where teams representing opposing deities played, the priests basing their prophesies on which side won (sort of like basing government policy on the outcome of the Superbowl, but in a culture where all events were interrelated and had sacred meaning, somehow reasonable).

The **Temple of the Count** was used by Count Frederick

Waldeck as his living quarters while surveying the ruins in 1833.

The Museum has beautiful panels, ceramics and large clay cylinders believed to have been used as incense burners. You can walk beyond the Museum to the pool on the Otolom river. There is a path, once an ancient road, that will take you out to the highway if you want to walk back to your hotel. Listen for the roar of howler monkeys off in the jungle.

Getting to the Waterfalls

Hire a taxi to Agua Azul for about US $35, and stay there up to 3 hours. Or arrange a trip with either the Cooperativo de Collectivos Chambalu or the travel agency Anfitriones Turísticos de Chiapas on Calle Juárez. A trip for up to ten people is US $35 and takes about 6 hours.

Agua Azul

We've never managed to take a photograph that does Agua Azul (blue water) justice, and we challenge you to try. This is one of Nature's masterpieces: a confluence of two rivers in a series of magnificent waterfalls. Follow the path along the banks of the river, swim in the large pools, loll in the little pools, or test your balance walking across one of the falls.

In-Tour Extensions: Bonampak and Yaxchilán

These important Mayan ruins, which until recently were only accessible by chartered airplane, can now be reached with relative ease. We emphasize the word "relative." The drive is not feasible during the rainy season (roughly June through October). If you have the time, we recommend that you see these ruins now. It may not be possible to visit Yaxchilán in the future as the Mexican and Guatemalan governments are planning a joint project to dam the Usamacinta River. Hydroelectric dams may flood many important Mayan ruins, including Yaxchilán and Piedras Negras. (See the October 1985 *National Geographic* magazine.) On top of that, the extensive Mexican rain forest is being clear-cut to provide grazing land. This entire magnificent jungle may soon be lost.

Getting There: A trip to either Bonampak or Yaxchilán from Palenque takes one very long day, a 9- or 10-hour round trip over rough dirt roads. At the time of this writing, the road into Bonampak was caved in, and we walked six miles in to the ruin. The hike took 4 to 5 hours. You'll want at least an hour at the ruins. The trip to Yaxchilán takes one-and-a-half hours round trip in a riverboat on the Usumacinta River. We wouldn't want to spend any less than two hours at the ruins, preferably three. To visit either ruin, leave Palenque about 5:00 a.m. and return by 8:30 or 9:00 p.m.

Why visit just one of these ruins when you've made it this far? We recommend two days for this side trip, with an overnight camp-out.

The travel agency Anfitrones Turísticos de Chiapas on Calle Juárez, corner of Allende in Palenque, offers a two-day trip that includes transportation, camping gear and meals. The cost is US $300 for up to six people, or US $50 apiece on a full trip. Call ahead from San Cristóbal to sign up for the next group (tel. 5-02-10 or 8-25-50). If your Spanish isn't good enough, have your hotel in San Cristóbal or a travel agent make the booking for you.

Bonampak: This compact ruin consists of one large mound, perhaps originally a single pyramid embellished with several temples and some carved stelae in the plaza. Bonampak is famous for its colorful murals depicting scenes from Mayan life. Over the years the murals were obscured by calcium deposits, and you were better off seeing the reproductions in the Museum of Anthropology in Mexico City. But the murals at Bonampak are currently being restored by field workers from the Mexico City museum. Now the restored portions of the murals glow in living color again, almost as if they had been painted yesterday.

Besides the experience of the ruins themselves, you walk through the rain forest to get there. We recommend an early morning departure if possible, since it gets hot fast in the jungle. It's a beautiful nature walk along a rutted road that deteriorates into a trail. Allow time to observe the busy work of the leafcutter ants and the myriad butterflies. You may be treated, as we were, to the sight of wild parrots in flight (remember your field glasses). You'll undoubtedly hear mysterious whirrings and thrashings off in the brush. Bring a plastic jug of water and replenish it at the compound near the ruins.

Yaxchilán: This was a ceremonial center during the Late Classic Period of Mayan culture (after 900 A.D.) Until a few years ago Lacandón Indians made pilgrimages here to make offerings and pray. It is an extensive ruin, in varying stages of restoration. Its majestic beauty is enhanced by the surrounding rain forest, and the site overlooks the broad Usumacinta River, the boundary between Mexico and Guatemala.

The locals at Frontera Corozal, the frontier town on the banks of the Usamacinta, provide transportation to the ruins in their long wooden pangas powered by outboard motors.

DAY 16
PALENQUE—MERIDA

After a last restful morning in Palenque you'll leave about noon to travel to Villahermosa and fly from there to Mérida, the Yucatán's largest city.

Suggested Schedule

9:00	A free morning for a leisurely breakfast, some time lounging around your hotel pool or a return to the ruins if you didn't get enough yesterday.
12:15	Bus leaves for Villahermosa to catch 3:55 flight to Mérida. Bus people will take a cab to the airport from the Villahermosa bus station. Rental car people don't need to leave Palenque until 1:00 p.m. to drive to Villahermosa Airport and turn in their car.
3:55	Aeromexico Flight #501 leaves for Mérida.
4:45	Arrive in Mérida. Rent a car at Mérida Airport or take a cab or colectivo to your hotel.
7:00	Have dinner and spend the rest of the evening people-watching in the zócalo or resting up in your hotel.

Mérida Airport
Before leaving the airport, make your reservations and/or buy your ticket home (Day 22). You may be returning via Mexico City or directly to your home town. The tourist information booth has a list of hotels and can assist you in calling for a reservation. The ticket office for colectivos and cabs is outside the front door of the airport. Buy a ticket to avoid being overcharged. There is a large selection of car rental agencies and some have specials. There is also a money exchange offering bank rates.

The Yucatán
The Yucatán Peninsula, commonly called the Yucatán, includes the states of Campeche, Yucatán and Quintana Roo. The peninsula juts northward from the southernmost part of Mexico and shares borders with Guatamala and Belize. You may feel as if you've been traveling south but, believe it or not, when you reach Isla Mujeres you are north of Mexico City, at about the same latitude as Guanajuato, and only about 90 miles from Cuba.

The peninsula is as flat as the proverbial pancake. Once while traveling with our Mayan friend Nacho Bey, who had never left the Yucatán before, we were amazed when he asked if the distant mountain range ahead was some sort of huge pyramid. He'd never seen a hill! There is very little soil on the peninsula, and the limestone bedrock is evident wherever you look. The limestone is perforated with caves, and all drainage is underground, so there are no rivers or streams on the surface. The *cenotes* (natural wells) you'll see all over are sinkholes that formed when the roofs of limestone caves collapsed.

The vegetation in the north is mostly scrub and low jungle. Most of the higher jungle has been cut for lumber. The local Maya still practice ancient slash-and-burn agriculture, eking out a living to the detriment of the forest.

Though the Yucatán countryside may not have the spectacular scenery found elsewhere in Mexico, the region offers an exciting array of Mayan villages, pre-Columbian ruins, beautiful beaches and unspoiled islands.

The climate of the Yucatán is consistently hot or hotter, with the exception of *nortes*, three- or four-day north wind blows, usually bringing rain. On the coast, March and April are windy months.

As recently as thirty years ago the Yucatán peninsula was all but cut off from the rest of Mexico due to lack of roads. The Mayan Indians of this region are proud of their cultural independence from the rest of Mexico. The Mayans here dress in traditional impeccable white clothing, and the dignity of their handsome faces is broken only by their broad, warm smiles and laughter.

Mérida

Mérida is a big city of one-half million that feels as if it were a smaller town in a different country. It is a very Mayan city. The Mayans are proud of their language. They are also very friendly.

Mérida was founded in 1542 by the conquistador Francisco Montejo. You'll see his name everywhere—from street names to a local brand of beer. Paseo de Montejo is a broad boulevard built in the 1890s, lined with mansions dating from the henequen boom. Henequen, a fiber derived from the sisal plant, was used to make rope and twine. Synthetic replacements have hurt the industry, though plantations still operate in the Yucatán countryside.

It is usually hot in Mérida, so flow with the tropical rhythm of the place and do your sightseeing in the cooler morning and evening hours. Reserve the hot afternoons for siestas or pool-sitting.

Mérida's streets are numbered in a simple grid system: north-south streets are odd-numbered and east-west streets are even-numbered. The street numbers are sequential, with the lowest numbers on the outskirts of town. Sounds easy, but when someone says the place you're looking for is "on the corner of Calles 58 and 59 between Calles 58 and 60," you'd have to be an international chess champion to visualize the location.

Accommodations

Mérida has lots and lots of hotels, with comfortable accommodations in all price ranges. Tina's favorite is the truly colonial **Posada Toledo** at the corner of Calles 58 and 57 (tel. 23-16-90). The dining room's ambience is elegant colonial, and the French suite is truly unusual. The **Hotel Casa de Balám** (Calle 60 #488, tel. 24-88-44) is also quite charming. The **Hotel Mérida Misión** (Calle 60 #491, tel. 23-95-00) is a deluxe hotel, often full.

Your best bets in the moderate range are the **Hotel Colonial** (Calle 62 #476, tel. 23-64-44) or the **Hotel Caribe**, pleasantly situated at the back corner of Parque Hidalgo (tel. 24-90-22). Rooms with air conditioning cost slightly more than those with fans. The **Hotel Colón** (Calle 62 #483, tel. 23-43-55) has air conditioning in all rooms.

The **Hotel Reforma** (Calle 59 #508, tel. 24-79-22) is a good budget hotel with pool. Don't take a room near the television. We were an involuntary audience to a loud late-night boxing match. The **Hotel Mayuc** (Calle 57 #481) has simple clean rooms, and the management is kind and helpful; no pool.

Food

Mérida is Steve's kind of town—lots of delicious food! The cooking of the Yucatán is famous throughout Mexico, and justifiably so. The blending of Spanish, Mayan and Lebanese cuisines makes for some truly interesting dishes.

For traditional Mayan food, try **Restaurant Los Almendros** (Calle 50-A #493 on the Plaza Ejorada). This pleasant restaurant serves outstanding *pibil* dishes (chicken or pork cooked in a fire pit and seasoned with achiote sauce) or their specialty, *poc-chuc* (thin pieces of grilled pork with a special sauce). The **Restaurant Colón** (Calle 62 #487) offers excellent regional food in a pleasant colonial patio.

For Lebanese food, **Alberto's Continental Patio** (Calles 64 & 57) is a good choice. Located in a beautiful old colonial house and patio, they serve steaks and pastas as well as Lebanese. **Cedro de Líbano**, a more moderately priced Lebanese restaurant, is located on Calle 59 between Calles 64 and 66. Our favorite "hole in the wall" Middle Eastern restaurant is **Restaurant El**

Arabe David (David the Arab) at Calle 61 #542. The decor is nonexistent, but the food is tasty and inexpensive.

The **Restaurant Flamingos** (Calle 57 near Calle 58) is clean, has fast service and specializes in seafood and regional dishes. An attractive restaurant with patio or inside air-conditioning is the **Pórtico del Peregringo** (Calle 57 #501), serving seafood, international and regional dishes. For French food, go to **Restaurant Vannig** (Calle 62 #480).

Restaurant Express (Calle 59 #502, across from Hidalgo Park) serves a good breakfast. Try huevos motuleños, a huevos rancheros variation.

DAY 17
MERIDA

Today you'll begin your explorations of the Yucatán by foot and old-fashioned horse cab. Get acquainted with the local flora and fauna at the Mérida Zoo, then take time out for a swim (practicing for your beach days).

Suggested Schedule	
8:00	Breakfast.
9:00	Walking Tour.
10:00	Shopping in market.
11:00	Horse cab to the Museum of Anthropology.
12:00	Lunch.
1:00	Cool off in pool. (Dedicated ruins-goers-see Alternate Plan.)
3:00	Visit the Zoo.
6:00	Dinner.
8:00	Ballet Folklórico.
	Alternate Plan
Morning	Same as above, but make tour reservations instead of buying tickets to Ballet.
2:00	Take Gonzalez Agency (Calle 59 #476, tel. 1-01-97) tour to Uxmal and the light and sound show, returning at 11:00 p.m. US $20 includes dinner.

Walking Tour
Start at the Plaza Cepeda Peraza, the original plaza of Mérida (also called Parque Hidalgo). Walk down Calle 60 to Calle 59 and visit the Templo del Tercer Orden. Stop in at the tourist office for brochures, tour information and maps. The Teatro Peón Contreras, on the next corner, usually has an art exhibit in the lobby. Buy tickets for tonight's Ballet Folklórico. Walk back along Calle 60 to the zócalo and check out the Cathedral. Continue south and make a left on Calle 65. At Calle 56A, turn right and a couple of blocks on you'll see a green cement stairway on the left leading up to the Mercado Municipal (city market).

Shopping Hints
Mexico's best hammocks are sold in Mérida. A word of caution: any hammock, correctly displayed, looks enormous. Many's

the unhappy tourist who strings his hammock up on his porch back home, gets in and finds himself precariously balanced on a net tightrope! Buy hammocks by weight. La Poblana, Calle 65 #492, gives good value, as does the store at Calle 56 #516. The weight of the hammock is listed in grams on the package in these stores.

Other good buys here are Panama hats, guayaberas and huipiles. The best quality Panama hats have a very fine weave and can be rolled up. Guayaberas, the dress shirt for work or pleasure, are worn all over Mexico. Huipiles are the beautiful white dresses of the Mayan women, colorfully embroidered with flowers. Shrewd bargaining is called for. Don't be embarrassed to offer ⅓ to ½ of the asking price. Shops all around the market sell these items.

Horse Cabs

The horse cabs weren't just "fluted up" for the tourists. They used to be the main means of public transportation in Mérida and are still used that way. The horse cab stand, marked "Coches Calasa," is right in front of the Correo on Calle 65. If more than one cab is available, compare the prices of several. An hour costs US $6. It cost us US $1.50 for the 20-minute ride to the Museo de Antropología.

Museo de Antropología

This beautiful former mansion at Paseo de Montejo & Calle 43 has a fine display of pre-Columbian artifacts. Open Tue.-Sat. 8:00 a.m.-8:00 p.m., Sun. 8:00 a.m.-2:00 p.m., closed Monday. Directly across the Paseo de Montejo from the museum is the **Restaurant Arrecife**, with delicious grilled meats. So handy if you're hungry.

Getting Back Downtown

Your cabbie may still be hanging around waiting for a fare. Otherwise, catch any city bus that stops at Montejo and Calle 41. Get off in front of the big white Congress building on Calle 59 a few blocks from the zócalo.

The Zoo

The Parque Zoológico "El Centenario" is on Av. de los Itzaes between Calles 65 and 59. Don't miss this collection of Yucatán's birds and beasts (as well as the obligatory elephants and giraffes). There's also a playground and rides.

DAY 18
CHICHEN ITZA

Today you'll leave Mérida and visit the Ma~~~
Itzá with its infamous sacred cenote, once t~
sacrifices. There will be time for a cooling sw~~. ~~.~ore you
head for Puerto Juárez and the ferry to beautiful Isla Mujeres
(island of women).

Suggested Schedule	
6:30	Leave Mérida for 2-hour bus or car trip to Chichén Itzá.
8:30	Explore the ruins.
12:00	Lunch and a swim.
1:30	Leave for Puerto Juárez by bus (Car people— see "Transportation: Isla Mujeres" below).
3:30	Arrive in Puerto Juárez, catch ferry to Isla Mujeres. Check into hotel.
7:00	Dinner and a walk around town.

Transportation: Mérida to Chichén Itzá
The Mérida bus station, Unión de Camioneros de Yucatán, is on Calle 69 between 68 and 70. Autotransportes de Oriente has a bus leaving for Chichén Itzá at 6:30 a.m. Buy your ticket by 6:00 a.m. Get off at the ruins, not in the village. For a small fee you can leave your luggage in a room behind the ticket office, marked "Salida."

Chichén Itzá
Chichén Itzá gets crowded. Leave Mérida early to enjoy the ruins in the cool of the morning.

Experts believe Chichén Itzá was founded around the time of Christ. An invading people known as the Itza (water witches or wizards) took over the city in the 4th century A.D. The name Chichén Itzá ("Well Mouth of the Water Witches") refers to the city's sacred cenote.

Sometime in the 10th century A.D. Chichén Itzá was influenced, and perhaps invaded, by Toltecs from the city of Tula near present day Mexico City. The Toltecs brought their own style of architecture and the worship of their God-king Quetzalcoátl (the Feathered Serpent), called Kukulcan in Mayan. No one knows whether Quetzalcoátl was a real person who lived at Chichén Itzá or a mythological figure who was already legendary when the Toltecs arrived. The Feathered Serpent was wor-

...ped alongside the Mayan Rain God, Chac, and many representations of both gods can be seen at Chichén Itzá.

From about 1200 A.D. to the 16th century, the Mayan-Toltec civil wars may have led to the fall of the Mayan civilization. When the Spaniards arrived, Chichén Itzá's people retreated to an island in Lake Petén in Guatamala. They remained there until 1697 when they were defeated and their territory captured by Martín de Ursua, governor of Yucatán.

Once abandoned, the city of Chichén Itzá crumbled into ruins and was quickly overgrown by jungle. Although never "lost" like other Mayan cities, Chichén Itzá's significance was unknown until the 1840s. U.S. explorer John Lloyd Stephens discovered the Mayan civilization at Palenque and other sites, then proved that Chichén Itzá had been part of a vast Mayan empire.

Walk through the Ruins

The ruins are open from 8:00 a.m. to 5:00 p.m. A store at the gate sells guidebooks, postcards and maps. You can hire a guide

Chichén Itzá

(US $13) for a 2-hour tour in English, Spanish or French.

Starting at the Castillo (castle) or **Pyramid of Kukulcán**, ascend the main staircase guarded by two gigantic stone heads of the Feathered Serpent. When you reach the top, take the opportunity to orient yourself with an overview from the summit. This pyramid, built over an earlier Toltec temple, is positioned so that on the days of the spring and fall equinoxes at 3:00 p.m. seven triangles of light and shadow appear on the side of the ramp, forming the body of a giant serpent. As the sun moves, the serpent appears to descend from the temple.

Next climb the **Temple of the Warriors**, where you'll be greeted by a reclining Chac Mool figure guarded by two more giant serpent heads. Chac Mool represented the messenger of the gods. His carved figure is found at many sites. At the rear of the temple a platform supported by small warrior figures is probably a throne or altar. Below, in the **Temple of 1,000 Columns**, are carved friezes. The original paint is still visible. Across from the columns is a marketplace complex. To the southeast is a steam bath used for ritual cleansing, healing and hygiene.

Northwest of the Temple of the Warriors, you'll come to the **Platform of Venus**, so called because decorative panels depict Venus emerging from a serpent's mouth. Between the Temple of Venus and the Tzompantli (Wall of Skulls), follow the road to the **Sacred Cenote**, where human sacrifices were made. In 1967 archaeologists dredged the well and found the skeletal remains of over 1,000 victims, mostly children. Also found were copper bells, gold-soled sandals and copal in braziers.

Return to the **Temple of Eagles and Jaguars** to contemplate creatures eating human hearts, then the **Tzompantli**, covered with symbols of death. Continue on to the large and impressive **Ball Court**. The game of *tlachtli* was played by trying to hit a rubber ball through one of the stone hoops without use of the hands. The winning team also "won" the privilege of being sacrificed to the gods. To the east of the Ball Court, see the beautiful serpent columns of the **Temple of the Jaguars** and the remains of a mural painting.

Returning toward the Castillo, take the path southwest past a much-needed refreshment stand. Continue on the path to the **Ossuary**, where seven tombs were found; the **House of the Deer**, and **Chichanchob** (meaning "little holes").

Head southeast and cross the path to Old Chichen. See the **Nunnery** complex, so named because it looked to the Spanish like a convent and because it was said that female priests used to live there. The "church" is decorated with three masks of the Rain God, Chac. By now, identifying Kukulcán's dragon-like countenance or Chac's up-turned hook nose should be a cinch. The east face of the Nunnery Annex is marvelously decorated.

On your left is the beautiful and impressive **Caracol** (snail), a Mayan astronomical observatory. This graceful building is the only circular Mayan structure known. Its four doors open to the four compass directions. A small spiral interior staircase, now off-limits to sightseers, leads to an observatory for the rising and setting of Venus, associated with the deity Quetzalcoátl/ Kukulcán.

If you have the time and energy, follow the path to Old Chichén Itzá and visit the **Temple of the Phalluses**, the **Temple of the Atlantes**, etc. The entrance at the base of the of the Castillo to the room of the Red Jaguar opens at 11:00 a.m. Stop by on your way out.

Lunch
Take a cab from the ruins to a restaurant. At the **Pirámide Inn**, not far from the ruins going toward the village of Pisté, a comida corrida is less than US $4 and typical Yucatecan dishes are about US $2. The use of the swimming pool is included with lunch. The **Restaurant Xay-B** in Pisté also has a pool. The Villa Archaeológico in the hotel zone also serves lunch.

Transportation—Chichén Itzá to Isla Mujeres
Buses pass through Chichén Itzá for Puerto Juárez every hour on the half-hour. Buy your ticket on the bus. There is frequent pedestrian ferry service to Isla Mujeres from Puerto Juárez. If you need more help or info, the tourist office information booth at the ruins is open 8:00 a.m.-4:00 p.m. every day except Friday.

Car People: The car ferry to Isla Mujeres leaves Punta Sam, 5 km beyond Puerto Juárez. You need to be there at 5:00 p.m. to catch the 5:45 p.m. ferry. It is only a 2-hour drive from Chichén Itzá, so drivers can spend more time in the ruins, take a longer swim or stop at Valledolid to see Cenote Zaci in town.

Isla Mujeres
The island is 5½ miles long and about a mile wide. It's a 45-minute ferry ride from the mainland.

Despite increasing tourism, Isla Mujeres remains a fishing village with a thin and often crumbling resort veneer. The fishing fleet still bobs in the bay, and in the evening fishermen repair nets in doorways. Local restaurant menus vary according to the fleet's catch. Strolling the small streets on a warm tropical evening, glimpse island home life through the open doors of small houses.

In 1527 a Spanish expedition, lost at sea for 21 days, sighted the island. Statues of Mayan godesses guarded the coast, so they named it Island of Women. The only evidence remaining today of pre-Columbian occupation is the small Temple of Ixchel on the southern tip of the island. Isolated Isla Mujeres was a haven for pirates, among them the pirate Mundaca whose hacienda was here.

Accommodations

The **Posada del Mar** is near the beach, and upstairs rooms have views of the sea and the mainland. (Av. Rueda Medina #15; Mérida reservation number: 26-04-22). The rather pricey **El Presidente Caribe** (tel. 2-00-29), on the island's prettiest site, is surrounded by water. It has its own aquarium with turtles and sharks, and a pet pelican. For a comfortable bungalow with fridge and a porch go to **Hotel Kin-Ha** (Carlos Lazo #1).

The best moderate-price deal is the **Hotel Berny** (Juárez por Abasolo, tel. 2-00-25); swimming pool. We also recommend the **Hotel Caracol** (Matamoros #5, te. 2-01-50). The **Hotel Rocamar** (at Nicolas Bravo y Guerrero, tel. 2-01-01) has balconies overlooking the rough sea on the eastern side of the island; make reservations.

The **Hotel Caribe Maya** at Francisco I. Madero #9 (tel. 2-01-90) is a good budget hotel, as is the **Hotel Osario** at Madero and Juárez (tel. 2-00-18). For the get-down budget backpacker, the **Hotel Pac-Na** on Matamoros offers dormitory accommodations.

Food

El Peregrino (Francisco I. Madero #8) serves a good meal and delicious cake. We also recommend the waterfront **Lonchería Miramar**, near the Puerto Juárez ferry dock. For a "Late '50s Mafia" atmosphere and a decent dinner, try the **Villa del Mar** at Rueda Medina across from the ferry dock. Our favorite hole-in-the-wall is **Carnitas Estilo Michoacán** at Hidalgo and Abasolo. The **Estrellita Marinera** at Juárez and Abasolo serves a good breakfast. But the best Mexican breakfast in town is in the market at the stand marked **"El Popular Nacho Beh-El Rey de los Tacos,"** where they serve authentic conchinita or pavo pibil between 6:00 and 9:00 a.m. (Better to get there early—it goes fast!) Beware the **Tropicana**, an attractive juice and sandwich bar. They charged us an outrageous US $2 for an ice cream cone.

Nightlife

La Peña, down from the Hotel Rocamar, has "Amigo Time" between 6:00 and 7:30 p.m. Nearby **Sergio's** also has a happy hour.

DAY 19
ISLA MUJERES

You have arrived! No heavy scheduling for today. Relax on the beach.

Suggested Schedule

10:00	Late and leisurely breakfast.
11:00	Hit the beach.
2:00	Late and leisurely lunch.
3:00	Loll around the pool or around your room.
5:00	Walk around town. Pick out a boat tour to El Garrafón for tomorrow and make your reservations.
6:00	Happy hour.
7:00	Dinner.
8:00	Hang out on the plaza.

Activities

Several places rent small motorcycles, mopeds or bicycles to buzz around the island. Motorcycles are US $10 a day, deposit required. Shop around—prices don't vary much but some machines are nicer than others. Rent windsurfing equipment and/or instruction at "Escuela de Windsurfing y Renta de Equipos de Deportes Aquáticos" down Coco Beach from Hotel Presidente. Boards are US $10 per hour, a 1 ½ -hour lesson US $25. They also rent snorkeling equipment, Sunfish sailboats, Hobiecats, kayaks, air mattresses, beach towels and chairs with umbrellas.

Scuba diving equipment, instruction and guided diving trips are offered by the "Diving Shop" in front of the ferry dock. The nearby Buceos de México also offers trips to Isla Contoy bird sanctuary, deep-sea fishing and diving. Next door, Isla Mujeres SCL has daily trips to El Garrafón, diving and trips to Isla Contoy. The most economical trips to El Garrafón and other attractions are offered by La Sociadad Coop de Lancheros. Their office is next to the passenger ferry dock. They have a colectivo boat trip to El Garrafón every morning at 10:30 a.m. for about US $6 per person.

Nightlife

There's something going on around the plaza on any evening.

DAY 20
ISLA MUJERES

More beaches and swimming today, as well as a boat ride to El Garrafón for snorkeling on the coral reef. In the late afternoon you'll visit the Mayan temple on the southern tip of the island.

Suggested Schedule	
9:00	Breakfast.
10:00	Take boat tour to El Garrafón for snorkeling and lunch. About 4 hours. (Alternate plan: ignore this—back to the beach!)
2:30	Cool off in the pool and write "Wish you were here" postcards to the folks back home.
4:30	Rent bicycle and pedal to the southern tip of the island to enjoy sunset at the Mayan Templo de Ixchel. (Or: Still at the beach? Rent a moped or taxi later for sunset at Ixchel.)
7:00	Dinner and pack up for early departure tomorrow morning.

Sightseeing Highlights
Templo de Ixchel—On the southern tip of the island, this small Mayan lookout tower is perfect for sunset-watching.
Coco Beach—The best swimming beach on the island. Sad to say, the coconut trees that give this beach its name died of disease. The beach runs along the northern end of the island between the Hotel Presidente and the lighthouse.
El Garrafón—This small swimming beach with coral reefs offshore is great for novice snorkelers. Schools of tropical fish thrive in the shelter of the reefs. There are snack bars and snorkel equipment rentals. It is a national park, and spearfishing is not allowed.
Playa Lancheros—This sheltered beach about 5 minutes drive from town on the way to El Garrafón offers sea turtle rides. We've seen the turtles tormented by people climbing on their backs to pose for snapshots. Please have some compassion for this endangered species.

DAY 21
XEL-HA AND TULUM

Today you will leave your island paradise. Console yourself
with a visit to the beautiful lagoon of Xel-ha, and continue on
to Tulum, a Mayan ruin on a bluff overlooking the Caribbean.
After touring the ruins, you'll proceed to Cobá, where you'll
check into an elegant hotel.

Suggested Schedule

8:30	Get your well-rested bones up for breakfast.
9:00	Be at the car ferry dock to buy tickets and get in line, should there be one.
10:00	Take car ferry to Punta Sam.
11:00	Drive to Xel-ha, lunch.
1:00	Drive to Tulum.
2:15	Tour ruins of Tulum.
4:00	Drive to Cobá.
4:30	Check into hotel, take a dip in the pool and relax.
6:30	Dinner at hotel.

Helpful Hints for Bus Riders

Catch the 7:00 ferry to Puerto Juárez. Take a city bus from the
Puerto Juárez ferry dock into Cancún. Ask to be let off at the
bus station on Av. Tulum and Av. Uxmal. Get your tickets for
Tulum at Autotransportes del Caribe and munch a breakfast in
the station. Catch the 9:30 bus to Tulum. You'll have a brief
45-minute visit to the ruins and be out at the crossroads in time
to catch the noon bus to Cobá. Check into the **Hotel Villas
Arqueologicas** (this is the budget traveler's big splurge on the
trip). Have lunch at the hotel or in the nearby village. Then tour
the ruins.

Xel-ha (pronounced "shell-ha")

A freshwater lagoon mixes with Caribbean salt waters to create
this natural aquarium and a snorkeler's paradise. Spear-fishing
is prohibited in this national park. In these waters we've seen
colorful parrot fish longer and a good deal broader than our
daughter. Snorkeling gear rents for US $3 a day, and underwater
cameras, kayaks and glass-bottomed boat are available. For
lunch, try the delicious fried chicken lunch at the **Bar Xel-ha**.

Tulum

Though archaeologists may sniff at this city constructed during the decline of the Mayan civilization, Tulum holds a powerful magic.

Perched on a 40-foot limestone cliff overlooking the blue-green waters, this walled fortress was first seen by Europeans in 1511. Two shipwreck survivors, Gerónimo de Aguilar and Gonzalo Guerrero, made it to shore and were enslaved by the Mayans. A few years later the chaplain of Juan de Grijalva's expedition described a walled city with towers that looked as large as Seville. Local fishermen told us that they find the entrance to the barrier reef by aligning their boats with the windows of the Castillo.

At the time of the Conquest, a series of forts along this coast protected the Maya from their primitive enemies to the south. The buildings face the southeast, accounting for its ancient name, Zama (place of the sunrise). The modern name, Tulum, means "wall," and indeed a wall protects the city on three sides.

Ancient Zama must have been an important trading port. Broad stone causeways, an ancient highway system, linked Tulum to Cobá, Chichén-Itzá and Uxmal. Archaeologists date the construction of Zama between 700 A.D. and 1000 A.D.

Walk through Tulum

After you pass through the protective wall, the first building on your right, **Structure 20**, probably a palace, has traces remaining of wall paintings. Beside this building is **Funerary Platform 9**, in which a grave was found. Directly in front of #20 is the **Temple of the Frescoes**, Tulum's best preserved temple. Inside are the remains of some excellent murals. The center niche over the pillars of the gallery preserves an image of the "Descending God." Continuing toward the sea, you come to the Dance Platform in front of the **Castillo**, the largest building at Tulum. The three entrances to the temple at the top of the stairway are flanked by the usual serpent columns of the god Kukulcán. The building immediately to the right of the Castle is called the **Temple of the Initial Series**. Our favorite view of Tulum and its coast is south on the point in front of the remains of **Temple 54**. To the immediate left (northeast) of the Castle is the **Temple of the Descending God**. Continuing north, you come to the **Snail Platform**, named for the shells of giant sea snails that were found here. Zig out to **Temple 45** on the cliff for another view of the coast, and zag back to the **House of the Cenote**, the temple built above the cave that was Tulum's natural storage tank for rainwater. Your vaguely counterclockwise circle takes you to **Structure 34** and the **Great Platform**, and **Palace 25** and the **Great Palace**.

The ruins are open from 8:00 a.m. to 5:00 p.m. daily. English speaking guides are available.

Food and Accommodations in Cobá

We're only recommending one hotel—because there aren't any others. Determined budget travelers can probably find a room in the village, but why not treat yourself to luxury as you near your trip's end? On a lovely lake shore, the **Hotel Villas Arqueológicas** offers exceptional accommodations for about US $20 per person. It is within walking distance of the ruins. For reservations, write Hotel Villas Arqueológicas, APDO 710, Cancún, Quintana Roo, Mexico.

DAY 22
COBA-RETURN TO MERIDA

Suggested Schedule	
9:00	Breakfast in hotel.
10:00	Walk to and through Cobá ruins.
1:00	Return to hotel for lunch.
2:00	Drive to Mérida via Valladolid.
5:00	Arrive in Mérida and check into a hotel.
6:00	Last dinner in Mexico—Make it a good one!

Helpful Hints for Bus Riders
A bus leaves for Valladolid at noon; get details from the hotel.

Cobá
Cobá is a Classic site (600-900 A.D.) and thus pre-dates both Tulum and Chichén Itzá. Its construction style resembles the Mayan ruins of the Petén in Guatamala.

The least explored and reconstructed ruin on your itinerary, Cobá gives a sense of the tremendous power of the jungle to undo the work of humans. Cobá was once the hub of a network of roads, called *sacbes*, that connected the Mayan peninsular cities. The site extends almost 12 miles and is believed to have more than 6,500 structures. Such is the encroachment of the jungle that less than half of the roads are traceable today, even with aerial mapping.

Walk through Cobá
Immediately upon entering the ruins, take the well-marked pathway to the right to the **Cobá Group.** There is a small ball court and a large pyramid called the Iglesia (church) with a stelae (carved stone slab) at the foot of the stairs. Returning to the main path, you'll pass the **Chumuc Mul Group** on your left, still undeveloped. Taking the next well-marked path to the right brings you to the **Las Pinturas** group, so called because the building on top of the pyramid has paintings on the front. Continuing on the path south, you'll come to Macanxoc Lake and the **Macanxoc Group**, well-preserved stelae. There are also the remains of an old Mayan road. Return to the main path, turn right and you'll come to the **Nohoch Mul Group** on the left. 120 steps to the top of northern Yucatán's tallest pyramid are rewarded by an outstanding view of the surrounding jungle. The temple holds three figures of the Descending God. To the

northwest is a view of the **Great Platform**. Descend from the pyramid and visit Stelae #20 in front of **Temple 10**.

Return to Mérida
The new road to Valladolid saves a lot of driving time. Check into your favorite hotel and enjoy a tasty Yucatecan dinner.

Airport Hint
Save out enough pesos for the airport exit tax. The amount of the tax, about US $10, is subject to change. Inquire at your hotel.

POST-TOUR OPTIONS

MEXICO CITY

In our 22-Day tour itinerary, we've only skimmed the surface of what this tremendous city has to offer. If you have extra time, you may want to spend a couple more days here on your way home.

Check the *Mexico City Daily Bulletin* and you'll find 8 pages of gallery and exhibit listings—something for everybody. The Federal Power Commission Technology Museum, for example, recently exhibited works from the northern state of Coahuila. We could kick ourselves for not getting to the Museum of Corruption while it was open.

Not listed in the *Daily Bulletin*, but of particular interest to Diego Rivera fans, is the Secretaria de Educación Pública building with over 200 Rivera murals. At Calle Argentina #28 not far from the Zócalo, the building is open from 8:00 a.m. to 8:00 p.m., Mon.-Fri.

Coyoacán and University City

A 30-minute taxi ride south from the Zócalo, the National University of Mexico is the oldest school of higher learning in the Americas, chartered in 1551. The buildings themselves are monumental works of art, covered with murals designed by Juan O'Gorman, David Siqueiros, Jose Morado and Francisco Helguera.

15 minutes away in Coyoacan is the Frida Kahlo Museum (corner of Allende and Londres at #247), the former home of Frida Kahlo and her husband Diego Rivera. Visit the Anahuacalli-Diego Rivera Museum, displaying the artist's collection of pre-Columbian art (Calle Museo #150). Leon Trotsky's home is in the same area at Viena #45.

Xochimilco (pronounced So-chee-meel-co)

Go on a Sunday when these floating gardens are crowded with boats full of families out for picnics. There are boatloads of musicians for hire by the song or by the hour, or, like Garibaldi Square, you can freeload it and just enjoy the music in passing. You can bargain for a barge to float you through the canals— a sample of the intricate waterways of Tenochtitlan before the conquest, when landfills of mud and reed were used for cultivation. Taxi is the easiest way to get there.

La Villa de Guadalupe

After the Conquest, the Archbishop of Mexico ordered all pagan shrines destroyed. These included the shrine of the Aztec goddess of earth and corn, Tonantzin (the virgin and little mother) on Tepeyac Hill near the capital. On Dec. 9, 1531, on this same hill, the Virgin Mary appeared to Juan Diego, a poor Indian convert. She told him that she wanted a church built on the site. And so this dark-skinned Virgin replaced the Aztec goddess.

In 1976 a huge modern basilica was built to exhibit Juan Diego's cloak miraculously imprinted with the Virgin's image. The original Spanish church nearby is now a museum. This is Mexico's most sacred shrine. Take Metro Line 3 to the "Basilica" stop.

TAXCO

Taxco is only a little over 100 miles (3 hours' drive) from Mexico City, in the state of Guerrero, and can be reached easily by bus or rental car. The town is famous for silver jewelry. Sterling silver will be stamped with the number "922," signifying that it is 92.2% pure silver.

The town is built on a mountainside. Be prepared to climb steep, narrow cobblestone streets. If you're driving, park on or near the highway that runs along the bottom of the town.

Taxco is a tourist town, with an array of restaurants and hotels to choose from. Guides steer you to stores that pay them commissions, raising the price of what you buy. The town is not large, so there's no problem exploring it on your own. Check out the market in the lower section of town. It's built in layers up the hill, some of it on the stairways.

Getting there: If you're driving, take the toll road (95D) out of Mexico City toward Cuernavaca. Head south toward Acapulco until you see signs for Taxco. To go by bus, take the Metro to Mexico City's "Terminal Central de Autobuse del Sur" (Calzada Tlalpan #2205, "Taxquena" Metro station). Estrella de Oro is the first-class line serving Taxco. Flecha Roja offers second-class service. You can also take a tour. Check with a travel agency or ask at your hotel.

PACIFIC BEACHES

Manzanillo

Mexico's major west coast port has recently become a tourist center. This funky, crowded, hot little town contrasts with an incredible jet-set resort, Las Hadas ("the fairies"), located across Manzanillo Bay. Built by Bolivian tin magnate Antenor Patino, Las Hadas is worth visiting for a drink and a swim even if you don't intend to stay there.

You'll find a number of hotels and bungalows in the Las Brisas beach area north of town along Manzanillo Bay. The beach at Las Brisas is steep and not as good for swimming as other beaches a little further north on Santiago Bay, which also offers several hotel choices.

Manzanillo can be reached by air from most major cities in both Mexico and the U.S. The international airport is 30 miles north of town. Colectivos and taxis, as well as local buses, make frequent trips from the airport into the city and to nearby resorts. You can also reach Manzanillo by train, with daily departures from Guadalajara, or on numerous first and second class bus lines. It's about a six-hour trip by car or bus from Guadalajara; the train takes twice as long.

Barra de Navidad and Melaque (San Patricio)

Melaque and Barra de Navidad are two small beach towns about 35 miles up the coast from Manzanillo. They are so close together as to be practically one town, and it's a pleasant walk along the beach between the two. On weekends and holidays, people from Guadalajara come in droves. During the week it's usually quiet.

The beaches are fine, and moderately-priced hotels, bungalows and good seafood restaurants abound. Barra has more and better restaurants. Melaque is at the more sheltered end of the bay, its beach is less sloped and the water is calmer for swimming.

The beach restaurants of Barra are a good place to experience Seafood Sunday. Huge extended families and groups of friends gather for an afternoon of eating, drinking and music provided by local mariachi bands. You may be offered drinks and plates of shrimp and other delicacies. Mexicans are amazingly hospitable and often invite passing tourists to join their picnics and family get-togethers.

Getting there: There is frequent service by bus, colectivo or taxi from Manzanillo International Airport to both towns. Buses also run from Guadalajara (about a 6-hour trip) and Puerto Vallarta (about 3 hours). The towns are an easy bus or taxi trip from Manzanillo. Colectivos and local buses run frequently between Barra and Melaque.

Puerto Vallarta

With a population of 120,000, Puerto Vallarta (or "P.V.," as local gringos call it) is one of Mexico's most popular tourist centers. Prices are high, and it can be crowded. Tourism has brought a wide selection of excellent restaurants and lots of nightlife, as well as a large (if somewhat overpriced) selection of arts and crafts from all over Mexico, which is more than can be said for Acapulco or Cancún.

The small beach towns of Sayutla and Rincon de Guayabitos a few miles north of Puerto Vallarta offer a less expensive, more tranquil haven. There's not much happening except the ocean.

Getting there: There is frequent bus service from Guadalajara and Tepic to P.V. The roads are in good condition. There is an international airport with flights arriving from many Mexican and U.S. cities.

Ferry to Baja California

If you go to Puerto Vallarta, you can continue by ferry to Cabo San Lucas on the southern end of the Baja California peninsula. California and west coast residents with extra time can return home by this route, flying from La Paz to Tijuana or Los Angeles. (Note: Hotels and meals are considerably more expensive in Baja than on the Mexican mainland.)

The ferry, operated by the Mexican government, leaves Puerto Vallarta twice a week for the 24-hour trip to Cabo San Lucas. Check at the ferry terminal on the northern outskirts of Puerto Vallarta for current schedules and inquire on time to purchase tickets. We have taken this ferry many times and the procedure has never been the same twice. The ferry takes cars as well as foot passengers and the number of staterooms is limited, so get in line early to assure that you get a cabin. Cabins come in three classes: "Especial," the most luxurious with bath and sitting space; "Cabina," with two bunks and a bath; and "Turista" with two bunks and the bath down the hall. If you are traveling alone you may be asked to share a stateroom with a stranger of the same sex. If there are no berths available you can go "Salón" class but this requires sitting up all night in an airline-type chair or throwing down a sleeping bag and sleeping on the deck. Meals are served in both a dining room and a cafeteria. The meals in the dining room are acceptable but expensive by Mexican standards and the cafeteria meals are not recommended. We always pack a lunch and take fruit, snacks, canned juice and sodas.

The ferry trip with stateroom is very inexpensive. On our last trip the "Cabina" class for two cost only US $6.

PRACTICAL EXTRAS

Culture Shock
A Mexican travel experience can be overwhelming. Total im-
mersion into a foreign language can be like a plunge into icy
water. Help! you gulp as you grope madly for your phrasebook.
Then you realize you took the wrong turn a few blocks back
and you're hopelessly lost . . .

Sudden panic is one form of culture shock. If it happens to
you, sit down on a park bench or in a restaurant. Sit on the curb
if you have to. There's nothing like getting your body a little
closer to the earth ("grounding") to calm you down. Have a
familiar Coca-Cola or cup of coffee and a snack, and sit back
and watch life going on around you for a little while. This may
be the perfect opportunity to observe everyday Mexican life.
Practice your Spanish on the little boy selling *chicles* (chewing
gum). Get out your map and phrasebook and ask a waiter or
passerby for directions.

Homesickness is also a form of culture shock. If you've never
been homesick before, you may not even recognize the symp-
toms. A friend, new to Mexico, had been acting unhappy and
out of sorts for several days. He was suddenly himself again,
while pushing a shopping cart through a mall; the familiarity of
the surroundings had brought about the transformation.

Stay in hotels you like. If your budget calls for the cheaper
hotel, but you don't feel comfortable when you look at the
room, splurge. Take a room you like better in a slightly more expensive hotel. Your hotel room is your temporary home, your
retreat from stress, a place to nurture yourself—so do right by
yourself.

Long Distance Telephone Calls: You can often make calls
to the U.S. from your hotel room, or at least from the desk in
the lobby. To phone home during your trip, we recommend
you ask at your hotel for the particulars

Speaking Spanish
Language is like money. There's a great difference between a
small amount and none at all.

If you took two semesters of high school Spanish once-upon-
a-time, brush up. Take a class with a Spanish-speaking instruc-
tor or hire a freelance tutor. If that's impractical, get some
language study materials from your library or bookstore.
Among the best self-teaching books is *Spanish Made Simple* by
Eugene Jackson and Antonio Rubio (Doubleday & Co., $4.95).
Starting at least a month to six weeks before your trip,

work on your Spanish for an hour every day.

To practice hearing and speaking basic Spanish, try Berlitz' *Spanish for Travelers* (Latin American edition—60-minute cassette and phrasebook), or *Spanish Language 30* (90-minute cassette and phrasebook) from Educational Services Teaching Cassettes. Both are great for joggers, or for popping into your dashboard tape deck while you drive to work.

Most important, *try to communicate!* Any effort at communication will be richly rewarded, as Mexicans meet your attempts with a sympathetic ear and a big smile.

On a bus trip through Mexico a friend was doing his utmost to be polite and communicative with the Indians. One day as we struggled toward the exit on a packed bus, Steve overheard him exclaiming, *"Escusado! Escusado!"* to alarmed-looking passengers. He thought he was saying "Excuse me!", but was actually calling out, "Bathroom! Bathroom!"

Pronunciation Guide

Once you learn the vowel sounds in Spanish, you can pronounce most words you see written. Each vowel has only one sound, and the sounds of most consonants are similar to English.

Vowels:

A is a "short a" (as in F**A**THER)
E sounds like "eh" (as in **E**RROR)
I sounds like "ee" (as in POL**I**CE)
O is a "long o" (as in G**O**)
U sounds like "oo" (as in R**U**IN)

Consonants that are different than in English:
ñ sounds like "ny" (*cañon* = "canyon")
ll sounds like "y" (*llama* = "yama")
rr is trilled
g sounds like "h" (except when followed by a "u")
    "gu . . ." is pronounced like an English hard "g"
h is always silent (*hola* = "ola")
qu sounds like an English "k" (*que* = "kay")

Pronounce all syllables distinctly. Words ending in a vowel are accented on the next-to-last syllable, and those ending in a consonant are usually accented on the last syllable. A written accent mark shows that the word is accented differently than this general rule.

Vocabulary and Handy Phrases

Getting around

Where is. . .? ¿Dónde está. . .?

I want a ticket to. . . Quiero un boleto a . . .

How much is a ticket to. . .? ¿Cuánto cuesta un boleto a . . .?

I want to make a reservation.
Quiero hacer una reservación.

Which bus line goes to _____?
¿Cuál línea tiene servicio a _____?

What is the number of the bus?
¿Qué es el numero del autobús?

What time does the plane (bus, train) leave?
¿A qué hora sale el avión (camión, tren)?

Where does it leave from? ¿De dónde sale?

Where does this bus go? ¿Dónde va este autobús?

Does this bus go to _____? ¿Se va este autobús a
_____?

How many hours to _____? ¿Cuántas horas a _____?

How much time do we have here? ¿Cuánto tiempo
tenemos aquí?

Let me off at the corner (. . . here). Quiero bajar en la es-
quina (. . . aquí).

What will you charge to take me to _____? ¿Cuánta me
cobra llevarme a _____?

I lost my baggage. Se me perdió mi equipaje.

Where are you going? ¿A dónde vaya usted?

It leaves at. . . Sale a las . . .

ticket window caja (or) taquilla

reservation reservación

reserved seat asiento reservado (or) numerado

arrival llegada

departure salida

every hour cada hora

every half hour cada media hora

daily diario

passenger pasajero

driver chófer

line (or) **company** línea (or) compañía

to get aboard subir

to get off bajar

airport aeropuerto

bus autobús (or) camión

city bus (servicio) urbano

train tren

railroad ferrocarril

airplane   avión
first class   primera clase
second class   segunda clase
taxi   taxi, libre, coche (or) combi (or) coche de sitio
taxi stand   sitio
bus station   terminal (or) estación de autobúses (or) central de camiones
bus stop   parada
train station   estación de ferrocarril
ticket   boleto

Days of the week

Monday   Lunes
Tuesday   Martes
Wednesday   Miércoles
Thursday   Jueves
Friday   Viernes
Saturday   Sábado
Sunday   Domingo

Numbers

1	uno	**18**	diez y ocho
2	dos	**19**	diez y nueve
3	tres	**20**	veinte
4	cuatro	**21**	veinte y uno
5	cinco	**22**	veinte y dos
6	seis	**23**	veinte y tres
7	siete	**24**	veinte y cuatro
8	ocho	**30**	treinta
9	nueve	**40**	cuarenta
10	diez	**50**	cincuenta
11	once	**60**	sesenta
12	doce	**70**	setenta
13	trece	**80**	ochenta
14	catorce	**90**	noventa
15	quince	**100**	cien (or) ciento
16	diez y seis	**1,000**	mil
17	diez y siete		

Hotels

Do you know of a cheap hotel?   ¿Conoce usted un hotel económico?

I would like a room.   Quiero un cuarto.

 for _____ days para _____ dias

Do you have a room for two?   ¿Hay un cuarto para dos personas?

 a room with bath   un cuarto con baño

 with meals   con comidas

I want a quiet room, inside.   Quiero un cuarto sin ruido, adentro.

I want an upstairs room.   Quiero un cuarto arriba.

Do you have parking?   ¿Hay estacionamiento?

Is the car safe?   ¿Está seguro el coche?

Is there a night watchman at the parking lot?   ¿Hay un velador en el estacionamiento?

Do you have ice?   ¿Hay hielo?

hotel   hotel

motel   motel

inn   posada

bath (or) bathroom   baño

room   cuarto

key   llave

blanket   cobija (or) cubierta

double bed   cama de matrimonio

shower   regadera

hot water   agua caliente

fan   ventilador (or) abanico

air conditioned   aire acondicionado

manager   gerente (or) dueño

dining room   comedor

bar   bar

swimming pool   alberca (or) piscina

noise   ruido

Post office, Telegraph, Telephone, Bank!

I want _____ stamps for the United States.   Quiero _____ estampillas (timbres) para los Estados Unidos.

Three airmail envelopes, please.   Tres sobres aereos, por favor.

I would like to send a telegram to. . .   Quiero mandar una telegrama a . . .

I want to call the United States.   Quiero llamar a los Estados Unidos.

The number is. . .   El número es . . .

What time does the bank open?   ¿A qué hora abre el banco?
Can one cash a travelers check?   ¿Se puede cambiar un cheque de viajero?
What is the exchange rate?   ¿A cómo se cambia?
post office   correo
general delivery   lista de correos
letter   carta
address   dirección
envelope   sobre
stamp   estampilla (or) timbre
post card   tarjeta
telegraph office   telégrafos
telegram   telegrama
telephone office   oficina de teléfonos
telephone   teléfono
to call   llamar
a call   una llamada
number   número
operator   operador
long distance   larga distancia
collect   por cobrar
person to person   persona a persona
station to station   a quién contesta
credit card   tarjeta de crédito
Hello!   ¡Ola! (or) ¡Bueno!
money   dinero
change   feria, cambio (or) suelto
check   cheque
travelers check   cheque de viajero
currency (Mexican)   moneda nacional
dollars   dólares
bill   billete
bank   banco
teller's window   caja
signature   firma
money exchange house   casa de cambio

Mexican Food

Health: We once overheard some tourists in a trailer park offering their neighbors a cantaloupe which they had soaked in water with Clorox, saying they "thought it would be okay." We've met other Americans, traveling in giant trailers, who brought freezers full of food under the mistaken impression that it was unsafe to eat in Mexico. Some even brought a full water supply and went home when it ran out.

Only raw fruits and vegetables that you can't peel need to be soaked in water with water purification drops. In better restaurants you can trust the cleanliness, but if you want to be fanatically careful for the duration of the trip, you can swear off salads. The U.S. imports a good percentage of winter vegetables and fruits from Mexico, so you've probably been eating Mexican food at home.

Drink mineral water with your meals. *Agua mineral sin sabor* (mineral water without flavor) is a refreshing sugarless beverage. Brand names include Peñafiel, Tehuacan and Etiqueta Azul.

Tortillas: The tortilla is universal in Mexico, and once you learn that it often forms the bulk of a simple meal, you will leave a restaurant satisfied. You usually get a huge pile of tortillas with your meal, and you're free to ask for more—like coffee refills in the U.S. They also serve as eating utensils. It's considered polite and normal to scoop up your beans with tortillas, or create tacos out of anything on your plate using your salad as garnish. If you don't like tortillas, you can usually get bolillos, French style rolls. At worst, you'll be served pan Bimbo, the Wonder Bread of Mexico.

Every town has one or more tortillerías mass-producing tortillas for sale early every morning to lines of people with their baskets, towels and buckets at hand to carry home the daily stack. The tortillería of one small village we visit often now processes 5 tons of *masa* (corn flour) every day.

Comida Corrida: Restaurants throughout Mexico serve an afternoon dinner "special" called the comida corrida. Often the menu of the comida corrida will be posted outside the restaurant. With at least two choices in each course, it is a bargain. The comida corrida is traditionally served between 1:00 p.m. and 4:00 p.m. The comida corrida is prepared ahead of time. If you're in a hurry, it's the best choice.

Meats: The word *bistec* comes from the English word "beefsteak." In Mexico it means a slice or steak of any meat or fish, so

you can get *bistec de puerco*, for instance—"beefsteak of pork."
Chuleta means "chop" and may be of *res* (beef) or *puerco*
(pork). A *milanesa* is a thin steak of beef or pork, breaded and
fried like chicken-fried steak. *Asado* or *a la parilla* is "grilled,"
and *al carbón* is "charcoal grilled."

Tamales: Tamales come in many forms. (It is one *tamal*, two or
more *tamales*.) In the highlands the wrapping around the *masa*
(dough) is usually a cornhusk, in the tropical regions a banana
leaf is used. Fillings range from sweet to meat.

Chilies and Salsas: Mexico has an incredible variety of chili
peppers, and names for the same chili vary regionally. The common chilies are:
  Chile poblano—a long, dark green chili used for *chiles
rellenos* (stuffed chilies). Fairly picante to bell-pepper mild.
  Chile jalapeño—Fresh or pickled and canned. Approach
with caution.
  Chile serrano—Smaller and thinner than a jalapeño, it is
served in the same way and is commonly pickled and canned.
Fresh serranos can be real smokers!
  Chile habanero (Yucatán)—Beware, extremely picante.
Looks like a miniature bell pepper, but that's where the
resemblance ends. Its delicious and unique flavor should be
tasted with extreme care.
  Chile chipotle—a smoked jalapeñó in a rich dark sauce. It has
a unique flavor, usually quite picante.

Salsas (hot sauces): Mexican hot sauces fall into several
catagories. Uncooked salsa is made of chopped tomatoes,
onions and fresh chili peppers and cilantro (fresh coriander or
Chinese parsley). Cooked, this salsa is called salsa ranchera.
  Salsas are also made from dried chilies. Brick red and thin,
they may have seeds floating in them.
  A common salsa uses the *tomatillo* (green husk tomato) as a
base and may be either cooked or raw. Commercially bottled
salsas come in every imaginable flavor.

Will the food be too "hot" to eat? If you don't like hot
chilies and salsas, don't despair—you'll be able to eat in Mexico.
If you don't eat picante food, be careful of *moles*, chiles
rellenos, enchiladas (enchiladas suisas are usually safe), and
anything with *ranchero* (country style) attached to the name.
  Remedies: If you bite into something too hot, take a pinch
of salt. It's better to drink something hot, rather than a cold
beer or pop, to wash away the effects. Remember, unseen chili
juices remain on your hands and can burn other parts of your
body.

Central Mexico Food Specialties

Carnitas ("'little meats") are pork cooked in huge cannibal pots. You will see these big black pots in the streets of many small towns in Central Mexico; we can never resist stopping and buying some carnitas to go. Ask for *carne maciza* (lean meat) and avoid the fat, ears, tails and other delicacies so dear to many Mexicans. Carnitas make great picnic food.

Cabrito asado: Very young kid goat grilled over mesquite coals. So good it's definitely worth trying.

Pozole: This Mexican version of hominy soup may contain kidneys, livers and other meat.

Mole poblano: There are many different flavors of mole in Mexico (*mole* means "sauce" or "gravy"), but mole poblano is the most famous. It contains bitter chocolate as well as an indescribable combination of spices, herbs and hot chilies. It is an acquired taste.

Filete Tampiqueño: This "Mexican combination plate," consisting of a grilled flank steak served with enchiladas, refried beans, guacamole and rice.

Caldo Tlalpeño: This delicious soup of chicken and un-cooked avocado, flavored with the smokey chili *chipotle*, is often slightly *picante*, but delicious.

A Note to Vegetarians: Most larger cities and towns have at least one vegetarian restaurant and often a natural foods store where you can buy granola, whole grains, etc. Many restaurants serve meatless meals: cheese enchiladas, chiles rellenos, and of course the old standby, beans and tortillas. At the market, buy fresh fruits and vegetables, fruit *licuados* (smoothies), fresh bread and cheese.

Yucatán Food Specialties

The food of the Yucatán, a melting pot of Mayan, Caribbean, European and Middle Eastern cooking styles.

Sopa de lima: This famous Yucatán chicken soup gets its unique flavor from the juice of the *lima agria* (bitter lime)

Cochinita pibil: Pit barbecued piglet coated with *achiote* and bitter orange juice sauce. It is made into soft tacos or big sandwiches with *pan frances* (french bread). Addictive.

Pavo Pibil: Turkey cooked by the same method as described above.

Huevos Motuleños: this popular breakfast dish is similar to huevos rancheros, but more elaborate.

Huevos Malagueños: Eggs baked with shrimp and tomato sauce, garnished with asparagus.

Venado: Venison is commonly served in rural Yucatán restaurants.

Seafood:
Shellfish: *Camarones al mojo de ajo* (fresh shrimp sauteed in the shell with lots of garlic) is wonderful. Steve eats the crispy shells too. *Camarones al diablo* are similar, but with hot sauce, hence the name "of the devil." If you prefer the simple flavor of fresh shrimp, order them *al natural*.

   Seafood cocktails abound. Order them with or without *picante* and other flavorings. Mexicans often add cilantro (fresh coriander or Chinese parsley) to their seafood cocktails. If you have an aversion to this strong-tasting herb, be sure to order your cocktail *sin cilantro*.

   Fish: *Huachinango* (red snapper) is a popular dish in restaurants everywhere. It is often served in *mojo de ajo* (garlic sauce), *entero* (whole fried fish) or *filete asado* (grilled fillet). *Huachinango a la veracruzana* (red snapper Veracruz style) is fried and then simmered in a sauce of fresh tomatoes, onions, olives and capers. Other common fish are *sierra* (mild-flavored mackerel), *mojarra* (perch-like fish, often fried whole) and *lisa* (mullet), boney but tasty.

   Pulpo en su tinta: Octopus-in-its-ink is for the adventurous only. Great flavor if you can get past the tentacles.

Food Vocabulary
I'm hungry   Tengo hambre
I'm thirsty   Tengo sed
What is there to eat? (. . . to drink?)   ¿Qué hay para comer? (. . . para tomar?)
Are there beans? (. . . eggs?)   ¿Hay frijoles? (. . . huevos?)
I want . . .   Quiero. . .
We want . . .   Queremos. . .
The bill, please.   La cuenta, por favor.
We want to pay separately.   Queremos pagar aparte.
The meal was very good.   La comida estuvo muy sabrosa.
restaurant   restaurante, comedor, lonchería (or) fonda
menu   menú
plate   plato
an order   un orden
snack   antojito (or) botana
dessert   postre
beverage   bebida
fork   tenedor
spoon   cuchara
knife   cuchillo
cup   taza
glass   vaso

napkin servilleta
toothpick palillo
purified water agua purificada

Breakfast desayuno

bacon tocino
butter mantequilla
eggs huevos
   scrambled eggs huevos revueltos
   eggs sunny side up huevos estrellados
   hardboiled eggs huevos hervidos duros
   softboiled eggs huevos tibios (or) huevos pasados por agua
hot cakes hot kakes
jelly or **jam** mermelada
margerine margarina
toast pan tostado (or) pan dorado

Fruit fruta

fruit salad ensalada de frutas
fruit juice jugo de fruta
apple manzana
banana platano
cantaloupe melón
grapefruit toronja
lemon lima
lime limón
orange naranja
   orange juice jugo de naranja
pineapple piña
strawberry fresa
watermelon sandía

Vegetables verduras (or) legumbres

avocado aguacate
beans frijoles
   refried beans refritos
   boiled beans frijoles de olla
cabbage col (or) repollo
cauliflower coliflor
corn maíz
lettuce lechuga
onion cebolla
peas chícharos

rice   arroz
salad   ensalada
tomato   tomate (or) jitomate

bread   pan
roll   bolillo
sandwich   sanwich (or) torta

Beverages   bebidas
beer   cerveza
chocolate milk   Chocomil (brand name)
  hot chocolate   leche caliente con chocolate
coffee   café
  coffee with cream   café con crema
  black coffee   café americano
  coffee "au lait"'   café con leche (mixed with hot milk)
  Mexican style coffee   café de olla (with cinnamon and
sugar, boiled in a clay pot)
cream   crema
milk   leche
mineral water   agua mineral
  without flavoring   sin sabor
  non-carbonated   sin gas
soda pop   refresco
tea   té
  black tea   té negro
  camomille herbal tea   té de manzanillo
  lemon grass herbal tea   té de limón
wine   vino de uva
  white wine   vino blanco
  red wine   vino tinto

Meat   carne
steak   bistec
chop   chuleta
beef   res
chicken   pollo
  chicken breast   pechuga de pollo
  chicken leg   pierna de pollo
fish   pescado
ham   jamón
hamburger   hamburguesa
liver   hígado
pork   puerco
  pork chop   chuleta de puerco

sausage salchicha
  spicy Mexican sausage chorizo

broth caldo
soup sopa
noodles fideos
spaghetti, macaroni espageti, macarrónes (or) pasta

black pepper pimienta negra
garlic ajo
salt sal
sugar azucar

Crafts and Folk Art

One of Mexico's great natural wonders is her enormous variety of handmade crafts and art. There isn't a medium that the Mexican artisan has not explored—clay, wood, gourds, metals, straw, papier-mache, bark, seashells, textiles. The quality is equally varied, from Tijuana schlock to exquisite craftsmanship.

Mexico is a great place to do your Christmas shopping. American tourists are allowed to bring home $400 worth of goods per person from Mexico duty-free as gifts or for personal use.

Fonart is a chain of Mexican government craft and folk art stores. Prices are controlled, and you may find better deals than at retail stores.

Vendors will claim there isn't a shred of acrylic fiber in all of Mexico, or any polyester—it's all *pura lana* or *pura algodón* (pure wool, pure cotton). In the case of wool, look for the tell-tale glitter of acrylic blend in the sunshine. Polyester blends usually have a smoother texture than pure cotton, which is often a little wrinkled. If you're buying cotton clothing, remember it will shrink unless the cloth has been pre-shrunk.

In the Marketplace

How much is it? ¿Cuánto cuesta?
I can't pay that much. No puedo pagar tanto.
I can't pay more than _____. No puedo pagar más que
_____.
It's very pretty. Es muy bonita.
It's too big (small). Es demasiado grande (pequeño).
I don't like the color. No me gusta el color.
Will it shrink? ¿Va a recoger?
Won't the colors run? ¿No se manchan los colores?
Do you have it in pink (blue)? ¿Hay en color rosa (azul)?
I don't want it, thank you. No lo quiero, gracias.
I'm looking for a _____. Busco un _____.
What size? ¿Qué tamaño?
Won't you sell it to me for _____? ¿No me lo vende a
_____?
Where do they sell _____? ¿Dónde se venden _____?
market mercado (or) tianguis
store tienda
clothing ropa
pottery cerámica
weaving tejido
wool lana
cotton algodón
acrylic acrílico

hammock hamaca
basket canasta
folk art, crafts artesanía
mask máscara
jewelry shop joyería

Market Days

Mexico City:
La Lagunilla—indoor market, daily. Outdoor flea market in surrounding streets on Saturdays and Sundays.
Mercado Merced—daily
Mercado Sonora—daily
Ciudadela—daily
Xochimilco, D.F.—Sat. & Thur.

San Miguel de Allende—indoor market daily, street market Sun. & Thur., used clothing market Tues.

Guanajuato—daily

Pátzcuaro—Friday

Oaxaca:
Oaxaca city market—Saturday
Tlacolula de Matamoros—Sunday
Mitla—Sunday
Miahuatlán—Monday
Soledad Etla—Tuesday
San Pedro y San Pablo Etla—Wednesday
Ejutla—Wednesday
Zimatlán de Alvarez—Wednesday
Zaachila—Thursday
Ocotlán de Morelos—Friday

San Cristóbal de las Casas—daily except Sunday
San Juan Chamula—Sunday
Zinacantán—Sunday
Amatenango—Sunday
Tenejapa—Thursday

Mérida—daily

Isla Mujeres—daily

Fiestas

January

6—**Día de los Reyes** (Day of the Kings), all Mexico, Christmas gifts given.
17—Blessings of farm animals and pets.
20—**Día de San Sebastián**, Guanajuato.
20—**Fiesta de San Sebastián**, San Juan Chamula, Chiapas

February

2—**Candelario** (Candlemas, midpoint between winter solstice and spring equinox), all Mexico.
2—Native dances, Santa Maria del Tule, Oaxaca.
5—**Constitution Day**, all Mexico, national holiday.
7-8—**Festival of the Lord of Rescue** (local saint), Tzintzuntzan, Michoacán, fair with dances.
Week before Ash Wednesday—**Carnival**, most spectacular in: San Juan Chamula, Chiapas; Tenejapa, Chiapas; Zaachila, Oaxaca; Isla Mujeres, Quintana Roo; Mérida, Yucatán; Manzanillo, Colima; and Veracruz, Veracruz.

March

First Friday—**Festival of the Lord of the Conquest**, San Miguel de Allende.
21—**Benito Juárez' Birthday**, national holiday.
Week before Easter—**Semana Santa**, all Mexico. Good Friday is particularly good in Pátzcuaro, Mich., as are: Maundy Thursday in Tzintzuntzan, Mich; All-week celebrations in San Miguel de Allende, Gto; Corpus Christi—Mexico City, children bring baskets of fruit and food to the Cathedral to be blessed; Good Friday— Ixtalalapa, D.F., enactment of the crucifixion; Tuesday of Passion Week—Xochimilco flower fair.

May

1—**Labor Day**, national holiday.
3—**Day of the Cross**, all Mexico. Xochimilco, D.F., has a competition of flower-decorated altars. Big celebration in San Juan Chamula, Chiapas.
5—**Cinco de Mayo**, all Mexico, national holiday celebrating the defeat of the French at Pueblo.
15—Animals decorated, all Mexico.

June

10—**Día de San Antonio**: the following Sunday San Miguel de Allende celebrates this saint with the dances of *Los Locos* (the madmen) and a fair.

23—**Fiesta de La Olla** (Festival of the Pot), Guanajuato, Gto., serenades and dances.

24—**Día de San Juan**, San Juan Chamula, Chiapas, ritual horse races, processions.

July

First Wednesday in July—**Día de la Preciosa Sangre de Cristo** (Precious Blood of Christ), Teotitlán del Valle, Oax., processions and dances.

3—**Fiesta**, Oaxaca, Oax.

Third & Last Mondays in July—**Lunes del Cerro**, Oaxaca, Oax., Indian dances honoring the goddes of corn so she may bless the harvest.

16—**Día de Nuestra Señora de Carmen**, traditional dances in the barrio of San Angel on the outskirts of Mexico City.

24—**Fiesta de San Juan**, Palenque, Chiapas

25—**Día de Santiago Apóstal**, Tenejapa, Chiapas.

25—**Día de Santiago Apóstal**, Amatenango del Valle, Chiapas.

17-25—**Día de San Cristóbal**, San Cristóbal de las Casas, Chiapas, pilgrimages, candlelit vigils.

25—All Mexico, national holiday.

August

4—**Fiesta de Santo Domingo de Guzman**, Palenque, Chiapas.

10—**Día de San Lorenzo,** Zinacatán, Chiapas.

13—Mexico City, D.F., dances celebrating the defense of the Aztec city of Tenochtitlán against the Spanish.

15—**Festival of Our Lady of the Cibary**, Santa Clara del Cobre, Mich., fair and dances.

15—**Festival of the Assumption of the Virgin**, Santa Maria del Tule, Oax., procession, floral wreaths.

30—**Día de Santa Rosa**, San Juan Chamula, Chiapas, music.

31—Blessing of the animals, Oaxaca.

September

1-5—**Fiesta de Santo Domingo**, Palenque, Chiapas.

8—**Festival of the Birth of the Virgin Mary**, Teotitlan del Valle, Oax., procession and dances.

14—**Charro Day** (gentlemen cowboys), all Mexico.

16—**Independence Day**, all Mexico, celebration of the beginning of the War of Independence; fireworks and parades in Mexico City and San Miguel de Allende, Gto.

24—**Fiesta del Barrio de la Merced**, San Cristobal de las Casas, Chiapas.

29—**Día de San Miguel**, celebrated the following Saturday in San Miguel de Allende, Gto., bullfighting, fireworks, dances.

October

1-5—**Ferria de San Francisco**, Amatenango del Valle, Chiapas.
First Sunday in October—**Festival of Our Lady of the Rosary**, San Juan Chamula, Chiapas, music, costumes, dancing, market.
6-8—**Feria de la Virgen del Rosario**, San Juan Chamula, Chiapas.
12—**Columbus Day**, national holiday.

November

1-2—**Day of the Dead**, all Mexico, particularly spectacular on the island of Janitzio, Mich.
13—**Día de San Diego**, celebrated the following Sunday, Mexico City D.F., costumes, dances, fireworks.
20—**Anniversary of the 1910 Revolution**, national holiday, Mexico City: parade and sports exhibitions.
22—**Feria de Santa Cecilia**, San Cristóbal de las Casas, Chiapas.
23-24—**Fiesta de la Caridad**, San Cristóbal de las Casas, Chiapas.

December

8—**Festival of Our Lady of Health**, Pátzcuaro, Mich, Tarascan pilgrimage, dances, fair.
12—**Día de Nuestra Señora de Guadalupe**, patroness saint of Mexico, everywhere; Mexico City: pilgrims from all over the country flock to her shrine; dances; also rousingly celebrated in San Cristobal de las Casas, Chiapas, and Puerto Vallarta, Jalisco.
16-25—**Las Posadas**, Christmas season.
18—**Festival of Our Lady of Solitude**, Oaxaca, Oax., costumes and dances.
23—**Radish Festival**, Oaxaca, Oax., floral and food arrangements, figures carved from radishes.
24—**Christmas Eve (Nochebuena)**, all Mexico, processions at night, singing, family nativity scenes.
25—**Christmas (Navidad)**, national holiday.
31—**Procession of the Holy Sacrament**, Santa Clara del Cobre, Mich., torch and candlelight procession.
31—**New Year's Eve**.

Mexican Weather

1st line = average daily temperature
2nd line = average monthly rainfall

	J	F	M	A	M	J	J	A	S	O	N	D
Mexico, D.F.	54	56	61	63	65	63	61	61	60	59	58	54
	0.2	0.3	0.4	0.5	0.2	4.2	4.9	4.1	4.6	1.3	0.6	0.3
San Miguel del	57	60	64	68	70	69	67	67	66	63	61	59
Allende, Gto.	0.4	0.1	0.2	0.5	1.1	3.7	4.1	3.4	4.8	1.3	0.4	0.5
Guanajuato, Gto.	57	60	64	68	71	68	67	66	65	63	60	59
	0.5	0.3	0.2	0.2	1.1	5.4	6.6	5.5	6.0	2.0	0.7	0.6
Patzcuano, Mich.	57	56	61	64	68	68	63	63	63	61	58	55
	0.8	0.5	0.3	0.2	1.5	7.9	9.8	9.5	8.5	3.1	1.0	0.9
Oaxaca, Oax.	63	66	70	72	73	71	70	69	69	67	65	64
	0.1	0.1	0.4	1.0	2.4	4.9	3.7	4.1	6.7	1.6	0.3	0.4
San Cristobal	54	55	57	60	60	60	60	60	60	59	55	55
L.C., Chis.	0.3	0.0	0.4	1.4	5.1	10.0	5.6	6.3	9.9	6.0	0.9	0.6
Merida, Yuc.	73	74	78	81	82	81	81	81	81	79	75	74
	1.2	0.6	0.8	1.0	3.2	5.9	5.5	5.1	6.0	4.0	1.2	1.2
Isla Mujeres,	73	75	77	80	81	82	82	82	81	79	75	75
Q. Roo	3.0	86	1.1	1.2	5.5	7.0	5.1	4.2	5.5	8.4	3.4	3.7

ABOUT THE AUTHORS

Steve Rogers, formerly a biologist with the U.S. Fish and Wildlife Service, has been exploring Mexico since 1959. Steve worked with Carl Franz and Lorena Havens on the bestselling *People's Guide to Mexico* and is featured in many of the stories and anecdotes that have made that book so popular. Steve has immersed himself in Mexico over the years and has traveled to all parts of the country, hiked into remote areas and visited many different Indian groups and ruins.

Tina Rosa, a graduate of Stanford University, has been traveling in Mexico and the rest of Latin America since 1966. For the past ten years she and Steve have been collecting and importing Mexican folk art. Tina is a student of ancient Maya culture as it relates to ritual and spirituality, elements of which are explored on Steve and Tina's small-group Mayan Mystery Tours.

When not traveling, the authors and their 8-year-old daughter Churpa live in Oregon.

To Enhance Your Mexican Travel Experience
THE PEOPLE'S GUIDE TO MEXICO, Carl Franz' classic guide to the people, the culture and the land of Mexico has recently been completely revised and updated. **The People's Guide** is about living, traveling and taking things as they come in a foreign country. It's also about driving conditions and health and how to cross the border. It's about drinking the water without getting sick, and how to enjoy yourself regardless of how close you are to the nearest 'recommended' tourist attraction.

Harper's calls **The People's Guide to Mexico** "the best guidebook to adventure in the whole world." The Santa Fe *New Mexican* describes it as "more necessary than your toothbrush." Look for it in your local bookstore or order direct from John Muir Publications—and discover why travelers in the know would never cross the border without it.

Guided Tours
The authors of this and other JMP Travel guides lead small-group tours several times each year to update their books and search out new discoveries for the next edition.

If you prefer the convenience and security of a guided tour, here's your chance to travel with experts who "wrote the book" on the *real* Mexico. Explore ancient civilizations with Steve Rogers and Tina Rosa on their next **Mayan Mystery Tour**. Or experience Mexico's wonders on one of Carl Franz' and Lorena Havens' unique **People's Guide Tours**.

For free details, contact JMP TRAVEL SERVICES, P.O. Box 613, Santa Fe, NM 87501.

Travel Guides from
John Muir Publications

I'd like to order the terrific travel guides checked below...

Quantity	Title	Each	Total
	Europe Through the Back Door—*Steves*	$11.95	
	Europe 101: History Art & Culture for Travelers—*Steves*	$9.95	
	Europe in 22 Days—*Steves*	$5.95	
	Great Britain in 22 Days—*Steves*	$5.95	
	Spain & Portugal in 22 Days—*Steves*	$5.95	
	Complete Guide to Bed & Breakfasts, Inns & Guesthouses In the U.S. & Canada—*Lanier*	$12.95	
	Elegant Small Hotels—*Lanier*	$12.95	
	The People's Guide to Mexico (Revised)—*Franz*	$11.95	
	Asia Through the Back Door—*Steves & Gottberg*	$11.95	

		Subtotal	$
Non-U.S. payments must be in U.S. funds drawn on a U.S. bank.		Shipping	$1.75
		Total Enclosed	$

METHOD OF PAYMENT (CHECK ONE)

☐ Charge to my (circle one): MasterCard VISA

☐ Check or Money Order Enclosed (Sorry, no CODs or Cash)

Credit Card Number

☐☐☐☐☐☐☐☐☐☐☐☐☐☐☐☐☐☐

Expiration Date ☐☐–☐☐

Signature x _____
Required for Credit Card Purchases

Telephone: Office (___) _____ Home (___) _____

Name _____

Address _____

City _____ State _____ Zip _____

Send to: John Muir Publications
P.O. Box 613
Santa Fe, NM 87504-0613
(505) 982-4078

Please allow 4-6 weeks for delivery.